Editor
Eric Migliaccio

Cover Artist
Marilyn Goldberg

Editor in Chief
Ina Massler Levin, M.A.

Creative Director
Karen J. Goldfluss, M.S. Ed.

Imaging
Rosa C. See

Materials contained in this publication are copyrighted by Evans Newton Incorporated, 15941 N. 77th St., Suite 1, Scottsdale, AZ 85260.

www.evansnewton.com
© 2000-2008

Publisher
Mary D. Smith, M.S. Ed.

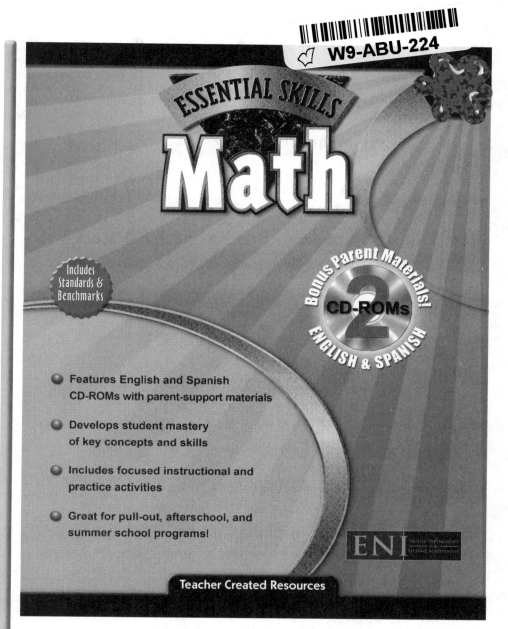

Developed and Written by

Evans Newton Incorporated

Teacher Created Resources, Inc.
6421 Industry Way
Westminster, CA 92683
www.teachercreated.com

ISBN-13: 978-1-4206-6213-7

© 2009 Teacher Created Resources, Inc.
Made in U.S.A.

Table of Contents

Introduction

The *Essential Skills* series was developed in response to an overwhelming number of teachers frustrated by the fact that their students didn't have all of the skills needed to be taught the on-grade-level standards. Due to this dilemma, the staff at Evans Newton Incorporated reviewed the standards from national organizations (NCTM, NCTE, IRA, etc.) and many states to determine the top prerequisite skills that a student going into a certain grade level should know, to be successful in that grade. The skills represented here are a compilation of many different states' standards and do not represent any one state's requirements. Since the introduction of skills vary slightly in some states, you may find it useful to also review and select *Essential Skills* books for the grade higher and the grade lower than you are teaching in addition to your own grade level.

The *Essential Skills* lessons were designed using the theories of many leading educational theorists. It is easy to see the influence of Madeline Hunter's *Essential Elements of Effective Instruction* used in the "Recall," "Review," and "Wrap-Up" sections. They were also designed using Grant Wiggins's Backwards Design Model, making sure the outcome and the assessment pieces were written before designing the actual instruction to go with them. In the questions included in the lesson, you will see many different levels from Bloom's Taxonomy represented, a reflection of the work of Benjamin Bloom.

As indicated before, the skills were written to cover skills taught at a previous grade level—generally just the preceding grade. The *Essential Skills* series was designed in a cumulative fashion—i.e., the skills from one grade level build on the skills from the previous grade level. If a student is multiple years behind, then going down to previous levels of the *Essential Skills* may be helpful. Please note that the lessons are meant to be review lessons that will help students activate prior knowledge. If students have never been taught the skill before, then the lessons will probably not be enough for the students to become proficient in the skill without further support.

Teachers from many different states and many different grade levels have found the *Essential Skills* to be very helpful at various times of the school year.

* Some teachers use the lessons at the beginning of the year to review important skills.

* Some teachers use the lessons throughout the year to introduce topics as they come up in their scope and sequence.

* Some teachers use the *Essential Skills* books for the next grade level following their state test as a way to prepare their students for the following school year.

In all of these situations, teachers have found the *Essential Skills* series to be helpful in building students' knowledge and preparing them to master the content that the states require students to know.

In addition to the classroom uses described above, books in the *Essential Skills* series have also proven to be effective tools for special programs such as after-school tutoring programs, summer-school programs, and Special Education programs, where teachers need to solidify students' skills and help them progress towards excelling at on-grade-level content.

We truly hope that you enjoy using the *Essential Skills* books with your students and find them to be highly useful, as has been the case with the many teachers who have used them before you.

Standards Correlation Chart

Listed below are the McREL standards for Math. All standards and benchmarks are used with permission from McREL.

Standards and Benchmarks	Skill # (Pages)
Standard 2. Understands and applies basic and advanced properties of the concepts of numbers	
• **Benchmark 4.** Understands the basic meaning of place value	Skill 23 (132-138); Skill 25 (143-145)
• **Benchmark 5.** Understands the concept of a unit and its subdivision into equal parts	Skill 17 (99-103); Skill 19 (110-115)
• **Benchmark 6.** Uses models (e.g., number lines, two-dimensional and three-dimensional regions) to identify, order, and compare numbers	Skill 20 (116-120); Skill 22 (126-131
Standard 3. Uses basic and advanced procedures while performing the processes of computation	
• **Benchmark 1.** Multiplies and divides whole numbers	Skill 18 (104-109)
• **Benchmark 5.** Performs basic mental computations	Skill 26 (146-150)
• **Benchmark 7.** Understands the properties of and the relationships among addition, subtraction, multiplication, and division	Skill 15 (90-93); Skill 24 (139-142)
• **Benchmark 8.** Solves real-world problems involving number operations	Skill 16 (94-98); Skill 27 (151-155)
• **Benchmark 9.** Knows the language of basic operations	Skill 14 (83-88); Skill 28 (156-160)

Standards Correlation Chart *(cont.)*

Standards and Benchmarks	Skill # (Pages)
Standard 4. Understands and applies basic and advanced properties of the concepts of measurement	
• **Benchmark 2.** Selects and uses appropriate tools for given measurement situations	Skill 8 (47-51)
• **Benchmark 3.** Knows processes for telling time, counting money, and measuring length, weight, and temperature, using basic standard and non-standard units	Skill 9 (52-60); Skill 10 (61-65); Skill 11 (66-70); Skill 12 (71-76); Skill 13 (77-82)
• **Benchmark 7.** Selects and uses appropriate units of measurement, according to type and size of unit	Skill 7 (40-46)
Standard 5. Understands and applies basic and advanced properties of the concepts of geometry	
• **Benchmark 1.** Knows basic geometric language for describing and naming shapes	Skill 6 (34-39)
• **Benchmark 2.** Understands basic properties of figures	Skill 5 (29-33); Skill 6 (34-39)
• **Benchmark 4.** Understands that shapes can be congruent or similar	Skill 5 (29-33)
Standard 6. Understands and applies basic and advanced concepts of statistics and data analysis	
• **Benchmark 5.** Reads and interprets simple bar graphs, pie charts, and line graphs	Skill 4 (23-28)
• **Benchmark 6.** Understands that data come in many different forms and that collecting, organizing, and displaying data can be done in many ways	Skill 3 (19-22)
Standard 8. Understands and applies basic and advanced properties of functions and algebra	
• **Benchmark 1.** Understands simple patterns	Skill 1 (6-11); Skill 2 (12-18)

Tables

Skill 1: The student will complete a two-row table given a rule or will find a rule for a given pattern.

Instructional Preparation

Duplicate the following (one per student, unless otherwise indicated):

- "Table Rules" reference sheet
- "Rules" worksheet
- "Patterns in Tables" worksheet

Prepare an overhead transparency of the following:

- "Table Rules" reference sheet
- "Rules" worksheet
- "Patterns in Tables" worksheet

Recall

Before beginning the **Review** component, facilitate a discussion based on these questions:

✻ Count by fives, starting with 25. (*25, 30, 35, 40, 45, etc.*) Write these numbers on the board.

✻ What can you say about these numbers? (*a pattern was formed, the numbers increase by 5, each digit ends in a 0 or a 5, etc.*)

Review

1. Write the following numbers on the board: 3, 13, 23, 33, and 43. Ask this question:

   ✻ What can you tell me about this set of numbers? (*they form a pattern, each number increases by 10, the digit in the ones column is always a three, etc.*)

   Explain that today they are going to find rules in patterns and fill in tables using rules.

2. Distribute the "Table Rules" worksheet and display the transparency. Direct attention to the "Words to Know" section located at the bottom of the page. Review the terms and definitions with the class. Continue to use and have the students use these terms throughout the lesson.

Tables *(cont.)*

Review *(cont.)*

3. Redirect attention to the top of the page. Have the students look at the table to the right. Explain to them that a table always follows a rule. To find the rule, you need to find out what happened to the number in the first column to make the number in the second column. Ask the following questions:

   ✳ What happened to the 1 to make the 6? (*Five was added.*)

   ✳ What happened to the 2 to make the 7? (*Five was added.*)

   ✳ What happened to the 3 to make the 8? (*Five was added.*)

   ✳ What happened to the 4 to make the 9? (*Five was added.*)

   ✳ What happened to the 5 to make the 10? (*Five was added.*)

   ✳ What is the rule in this table? (*Add 5*)

   Point out that each number in the first column is one number larger than the previous number. However, the pattern is found by comparing the numbers in the first column to the numbers in the second column.

4. Show the students the next table. Some of the numbers are missing in this table. Explain that to find the missing numbers, the rule needs to be found. Ask the following questions:

   ✳ What happened to the 24 in the first column to make the 16 in the second column? (*Eight was subtracted.*)

   ✳ What happened to the 22 in the first column to make the 14 in the second column? (*Eight was subtracted.*)

   ✳ What happened to the 20 in the first column to make the 12 in the second column? (*Eight was subtracted.*)

   ✳ What rule was used? (*Subtract 8.*)

   ✳ What needs happen to the 15 to find the first missing number? (*Eight needs to be subtracted.*)

   ✳ What number should be placed in the second column? (*7*)

   ✳ What needs happen to the 10 to find the second missing number? (*Eight needs to be subtracted.*)

   ✳ What number should be placed in the second column? (*2*)

   Point out that the numbers in the first column do not form a pattern. Ask this question:

   ✳ How do you find the rule, or pattern, in a table? (*The rule, or pattern, is found by comparing the corresponding numbers in each column.*)

5. Place the students in pairs. Distribute the "Rules" worksheet and display the transparency. Tell them that the first half of the worksheet is asking for the rule that was used to make the pattern. Have them write the rule on the line under each table. Explain that tables can be shown vertically as well as horizontally. Circulate to help pairs that are having difficulty finding the rule. When all pairs are finished, ask volunteers to write their rule on the transparency.

Review *(cont.)*

6. Focus attention on the second half of the page. Tell the pairs that for this section they need to complete the pattern by writing the missing numbers in each cell. Have them complete the first table, "Rule: Add 25." When they have finished, ask for a pair to share their answers.

   Now direct their attention to the table that says "Rule: Subtract 4." Explain that sometimes a number can also be missing from the first row in a table. To find the missing number, they will need to find the pattern that is shown using only the numbers in the first row. When they have found that number, they can then complete the missing numbers in the second row. Have the pairs complete this table. Ask for a volunteer to share his or her completed table with the class.

   Tell the students that sometimes a rule can have more than one part. Ask the pairs to look at the next table, "Rule: Double, Subtract 2." Explain that you start with the number 9 and double it (*18*), and then you follow the next part of the rule, which is "subtract 2." This gives you 16. Have the pairs complete this table. When they are finished, again ask for volunteers to share their answers by writing them on the transparency.

7. Focus attention on the blank table on the transparency. Have each pair decide on a rule and fill in all but three cells in the table. Have them exchange papers with another pair. They should complete the other pair's table and write the rule at the top of the table. When they have finished, have the pairs explain what was needed to complete the tables. Ask for some volunteers to share and write on the transparency the tables they made.

8. Distribute the "Patterns in Tables" worksheet and display the transparency. Read the directions as a class and have the students work on this individually. When they have finished, review the answers.

Wrap-Up

To conclude this lesson, have the students write a response using complete sentences to the following prompts in their math journal or on a sheet of notebook paper. Allow adequate time for task completion and then ask various students to share their responses with the class.

  ✳ How do you use a rule to complete a table? (*You use the same rule for each number in the first column to give you the number in the second column.*)

  ✳ When would you use a rule like this in everyday life? (*Answers will vary; they could include finding the cost of multiple items in a store.*)

Tables *(cont.)*

Table Rules

Look at the table to the right.

The first column shows the numbers 1–5.

The second column shows the numbers 6–10.

What happened to the number in the first column to make the number in the second column?

1	6
2	7
3	8
4	9
5	10

24	16
22	14
20	12
15	
10	

Look at the table to the left.

What happened to the 24 in the first column to make the 16 in the second column?

What happened to the 22 in the first column to make the 14 in the second column?

What happened to the 20 in the first column to make the 12 in the second column?

What rule was used?

What numbers will complete this table?

Remember: To complete a table, first find the rule.

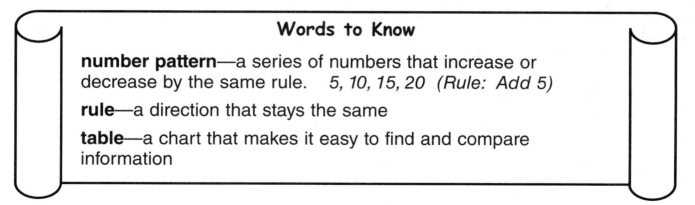

Words to Know

number pattern—a series of numbers that increase or decrease by the same rule. *5, 10, 15, 20 (Rule: Add 5)*

rule—a direction that stays the same

table—a chart that makes it easy to find and compare information

Name: _____

Tables *(cont.)*

Rules

Directions: What is the rule for each table?

1.

290	310
310	330
490	510
510	530
690	710

_____

2.

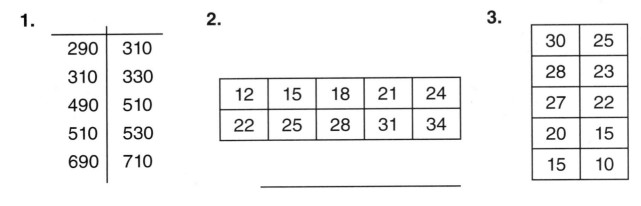

12	15	18	21	24
22	25	28	31	34

_____

3.

30	25
28	23
27	22
20	15
15	10

_____

Directions: Fill in the missing numbers to complete each pattern.

4.

Rule: Add 25	
200	225
250	275
300	325
350	
400	

5.

Rule: Subtract 4					
19	18	17	16	15	14
15	14				

6.

Rule: Double, Subtract 2	
9	16
20	38
21	40
25	48
33	64
40	
41	

7.

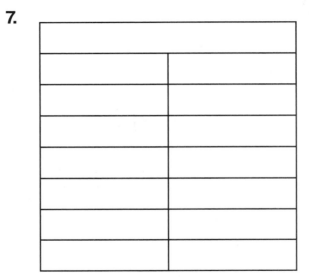

Tables *(cont.)*

Patterns in Tables

Directions: Write the rule on the line beneath the table. Then complete the table.

1.

112	127
122	137
132	147
142	157
152	

_____

2.

51	56
53	58
67	72
69	
74	
77	

_____

3.

30	33	36	39	42
34	37	40		

_____

4.

417	397	377	357	337
406	386	366		

_____

5.

93	92	91	90		
86	85	84		82	81

_____

6.

15	
17	
19	
21	
	35

_____

Number Patterns

Skill 2: The student will create, describe, and extend number patterns using addition and subtraction.

Instructional Preparation

Materials:

- cut out the "Rules" strips

Duplicate the following (one per student, unless otherwise indicated):

- "Number Patterns"
- "What Is the Rule?"
- "I Understand Number Patterns!"

Prepare an overhead transparency of the following:

- "Number Patterns"
- "I Understand Number Patterns!"

Recall

Before beginning the **Review** component, facilitate a discussion based on the following questions:

* What is a pattern? (*It is something that repeats; it could be made with shapes, colors, numbers, etc.*)

* Where have you seen patterns? (*Answers will vary. Examples: quilts, gardens, etc.*)

Review

1. Have five students stand side by side in front of the room. Ask the first student to hold up one finger, the second student to hold up three fingers, the third student to hold up five fingers, etc. Ask the following questions:

   * What do you notice about the number of fingers the students are holding up? (*Each student is holding up two more fingers than the person before.*)

   * What can the number of fingers the students are showing be called? (*a pattern*)

   Write this pattern on the board: 1, 3, 5, 7, 9. Have the students go back to their seats. Explain to the class that today they will be working with number patterns.

$$1, 3, 5, 7, 9 \ldots$$

Number Patterns *(cont.)*

Review *(cont.)*

2. Distribute the "Number Patterns" reference sheet and display the transparency. Direct attention to the "Words to Know" section at the bottom of the page. Review the terms and definitions with the class. Encourage the students to use these words throughout the lesson.

3. Redirect attention to the top of the page. Read the information in the "Rules of Patterns" section with the students. As they give the answer to each subtraction problem, write it on the transparency. Ask the following questions:

   ✳ What is happening to each of the numbers in this pattern to make the next number? (*Five is being added.*)

   ✳ What is the rule? (*Add 5.*) Write this on the transparency.

   ✳ What happened to each of the numbers on the board to make the next number in that pattern? (*Two was being added.*)

   ✳ What rule was used to form the pattern? (*Add 2.*) Write this on the board under the pattern.

   Have the class look at the "Extend the Pattern" section. Explain to the students that to extend a pattern they first need to find the rule that was used. Remind them that to find the rule they need to find the difference between each set of numbers. Tell them that since they know the rule is "Add 5," they now need to apply this rule to the last number in the series, 28. Ask the following questions:

   ✳ What is 28 plus 5? (*33*)

   ✳ What is 33 plus 5? (*38*)

   Write these numbers on the transparency and have the students write them on their papers. Remind the students that if the pattern is growing, using addition, or shrinking, using subtraction, the rule is always found by finding the difference between the numbers.

4. Ask the students to look at the "Create a Pattern" section. Explain to them that they are going to create a number pattern. The first part of creating a number pattern is to decide what the rule will be. For this pattern, the rule will be "Subtract 9." Tell the class that the second step is to decide on a number to begin the pattern. Explain that since this pattern is going to be subtraction, you need to start with a large number or your pattern will be very short. Complete this section by asking volunteers to explain how to find each number in the pattern. (*93, 84, 75, 66, 57, 48, 39, 30*) Write these numbers on the transparency and have the students write them on their papers.

Review *(cont.)*

5. Direct attention to the "Challenge" section. Give the students time to try this on their own before reviewing as a class. Then write the pattern (*14, 17, 16, 19, 18, 21, 20, 23*) on the transparency and have the students write it on their papers.

   Explain that when finding a rule to a pattern, it is important to find the difference between each set of numbers, since sometimes a pattern, like the one in the "Challenge" section, can have a rule that has more than one part.

6. Place the students in pairs. Give each pair a rule that you cut out from the "Rules" page and a "What Is the Rule?" worksheet. Have each pair create a pattern using the rule that you have given them. When the pairs have finished creating their patterns, have them exchange papers with another pair. The pairs need to write their names on the paper, find the rule that was used to create the pattern, and write it on the line. Then they need to extend the pattern by writing the next three numbers.

   When finished, the pairs need to get together to discuss how they found the rule and how they extended the pattern. Circulate around the room during this activity to ensure understanding. When the groups have finished, ask some of the pairs to share their patterns with the class.

7. Distribute the "I Understand Number Patterns!" worksheet. Have the students complete this independently. When the class has finished, display the transparency and review the answers as a class.

Wrap-Up

To conclude this lesson, have the students write a response using complete sentences to the following prompts in their math journal or on a sheet of notebook paper. Allow adequate time for task completion and then ask various students to share their responses with the class.

* How do you find the rule in a number pattern? (*by finding the difference between each set of numbers*)

* Where can you see number patterns in everyday life? (*Answers will vary. Examples: in aisles at the grocery store, in street addresses, etc.*)

Number Patterns *(cont.)*

Reference Sheet

Rules of Patterns

Look at this set of numbers. They form a pattern. 3, 8, 13, 18, 23, 28

Every pattern has a **rule**. How can you find the rule?

Find the **difference** between each set of numbers.

  ❋ What is 8 – 3?   ❋ What is 23 – 18?

  ❋ What is 13 – 8?   ❋ What is 28 – 23?

  ❋ What is 18 – 13?

Describe the pattern. What is the rule? _____

Extend the Pattern

Now, extend the pattern. What are the next two numbers in this pattern?

3, 8, 13, 18, 23, 28, _____, _____

Create a Pattern

Make a rule: "Subtract 9."

Choose a number to start from: 93

Subtract: 93 – 9 = 84. Then subtract 9 from the difference: 84 – 9 = 75

93, 84, 75, _____, _____, _____, _____, _____

Create a pattern using the rule "Add 3, subtract 1."

14, _____, _____, _____, _____, _____, _____, _____,

Words to Know

difference—the answer to a subtraction problem

number pattern—a series of numbers that increase or decrease by a rule that repeats

rule—a direction that stays the same

Number Patterns *(cont.)*

Rules

Add 3	Subtract 3	Add 4, Subtract 1
Add 4	Subtract 4	Add 4, Subtract 2
Add 5	Subtract 5	Add 5, Subtract 1
Add 6	Subtract 6	Add 5, Subtract 2
Add 7	Subtract 7	Add 6, Subtract 3
Add 8	Subtract 8	Add 6, Subtract 4
Add 9	Subtract 9	Subtract 4, Add 2
Add 11	Subtract 10	Subtract 1, Add 3
Add 12	Subtract 11	Subtract 6, Add 2

Name: _____

Number Patterns *(cont.)*

What Is the Rule?

Directions: Write your pattern on the lines.

_____, _____, _____, _____, _____, _____, _____, _____

- -

Name: _____

1. What rule was used to make this pattern? Write it in the box.

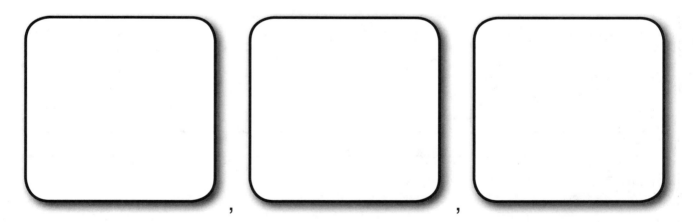

2. What are the next three numbers in this pattern?

[ ]   ,   [ ]   ,   [ ]

Name: _____

Number Patterns *(cont.)*

I Understand Number Patterns!

1. What rule was used to make this pattern? _____

> 4, 8, 6, 10, 8, 12, 10

2. What are the next three numbers in this pattern?

210, 190, 170, 150, 130, _____, _____, _____

3. What is the next number in this pattern?

19, 34, 49, 64, 79, _____

4. What rule was used to make the following pattern?

> 44, 38, 32, 26, 20, 14

_____

5. Create a pattern using the rule "Add 15."

_____, _____, _____, _____, _____, _____

6. Create a pattern using the rule "Subtract 4."

_____, _____, _____, _____, _____, _____

Organizing Data

Skill 3: The student will collect and record numerical data in systematic ways.

Instructional Preparation

Materials:

- butcher paper

Duplicate (one per student) and prepare an overhead transparency of the following:

- "Organizing Data" reference sheet
- "Which Shows the Same Information?" worksheet

Recall

Before beginning the **Review** component, facilitate a discussion based on the following question:

　✳ Why would we take a survey? (*Answers will vary.*)

Review

1. Ask the students what time they go to bed at night. On the board, write these times in a row. Tell the class that this information will be used later in the lesson. Explain that they are going to take surveys and place the information they collect in charts, tables, and graphs.

2. Distribute copies of the "Organizing Data" reference sheet and display the transparency. Review with the class the terms and definitions in the "Words to Know" section.

3. Show only the top of the transparency. Have one student read the first paragraph and have a different student read the information in the box at the top. Ask these questions:

　✳ How many more friends prefer the color pink than the color red? (*2*)

　✳ How many friends voted for either yellow or blue? (*9*)

　✳ How many more friends chose yellow than purple and blue combined? (*1*)

　✳ Is it easy to answer these questions with the colors written out this way? Why or why not? (*Answers will vary.*)

Uncover the rest of the transparency. Explain that showing the data in different ways makes it easier to read and compare. Review the tally chart, table, and bar graph with the students. Tell them that the same information is shown in each—it is just shown in different ways. Ask the following questions:

　✳ In which one is it easiest to see the color that was voted for the most? Why? (*Answers will vary.*)

　✳ In which one is it easiest to compare values to find the difference? Why? (*the table, since it shows actual numbers, it is the easiest to use to subtract and find the difference*)

　✳ Which of these representations is used to collect the data and record the information at the same time? (*Answers should include recording the information on a tally chart, since a tally is made for each vote.*)

Tell the students that each of these is correct to use to display the information. Their choice would just depend on how they wanted to use the information. Remind them that each can be shown vertically and horizontally. Draw a horizontal representation of one of them on the board as an example.

Organizing Data (cont.)

Review (cont.)

4. Have students look at the list on the board showing the times they go to bed. Tell them that you want to answer the following questions using this information:

   ✳ How many students were surveyed?

   ✳ What time did most of the students go to bed?

   Have the students help you decide if a bar graph, table, or tally chart would be the best to use to display this data. Create this on a blank transparency as a class, reminding students to use a title and labels (and on the graph, a scale). When completed, answer the above questions and ask for additional questions that can be asked and answered using this chart, table, or graph.

5. Place the students in groups of three. The members of each group need to decide on a survey question. Make sure they get their question approved by you so there aren't duplicates. The survey question could be about pets, brothers and sisters, favorite desserts, etc. When each group has chosen its survey question, have the groups take turns asking the class their questions and recording the information. Each group will be asking the class five questions about the information it has received, such as "How many more students have dogs than cats?" The group members need to decide the best way to display their data for the questions they will be asking. When they have decided on their questions, give them a sheet of butcher paper to create their tally chart, table, or bar graph to show the results of their survey.

   When the groups have finished, choose one group at a time to display its graph and ask its questions. When the members of each group have finished presenting, ask the following question:

   ✳ Why did you choose to show your data in this way? (*Answers will vary.*)

   After the members of each group have presented their chart, table, or graph, have them return to their desks.

6. Distribute the "Which Shows the Same Information?" worksheet. Read the directions with the class and have the students work on this individually. When finished, display the transparency and review the answers with the class (*A, D, and E*). Hold a brief discussion about how they chose the representations that did work and why others didn't. Then ask the following questions:

   ✳ Which item did Ben find the most of? (*pencils*)

   ✳ Which items did Ben find more of than erasers? (*crayons and pencils*)

   ✳ How many items did Ben find altogether in his backpack? (*30*)

   Remind them that the best graph or table to use would just depend on the situation. Answer any additional questions they may have.

Wrap-Up

   To conclude this lesson, have the students write responses using complete sentences to the following prompts in their math journal or on a sheet of notebook paper. Allow adequate time for task completion and then ask various students to share their responses with the class.

   ✳ Why is it helpful to place data in a chart, table, or graph?

   ✳ When would you use this information in everyday life?

Organizing Data (cont.)

Reference Sheet

Sometimes when you collect information, or data, it is hard to sort through and/or analyze the information. When the data is placed in an organized form, it is much easier to see and use the information collected.

> Amy asked her friends to name their favorite colors. She wrote down their answers: blue, red, yellow, yellow, pink, pink, blue, pink, purple, blue, yellow, pink, red, pink, purple, yellow, yellow, red, and yellow. It is *not* easy to analyze information when it is written like this.

She could show this data in a *tally chart*.

Favorite Colors

Color	Number of Votes
Blue	|||
Red	|||
Yellow	⊬⊬⊬	
Pink	⊬⊬⊬
Purple	||

She could show this data in a *table*.

Favorite Colors

Color	Blue	Red	Yellow	Pink	Purple
Number of Votes	3	3	6	5	2

She could show this data in a *bar graph*.

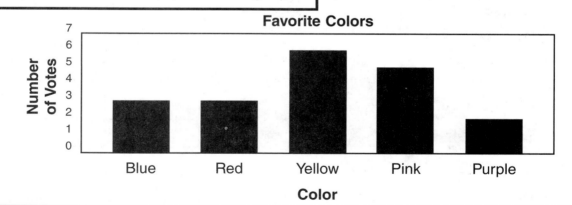

Favorite Colors

Words to Know

bar graph—a chart that uses bars of different lengths to show data.

data—information

table—a chart that makes it easy to find and compare information

tally chart—a chart that uses marks to record data

Organizing Data *(cont.)*
Which Shows the Same Information?

Directions: Read the situation. Shade in the box around the letter of each table, chart, or graph that shows this same situation in a different way.

> When Ben cleaned out his backpack, these are the items he found: pencil, marker, pencil, paper, gum, crayon, crayon, marker, crayon, pencil, eraser, pencil, crayon, marker, paper, eraser, eraser, pencil, crayon, pencil, marker, pencil, pencil, crayon, pencil, crayon, crayon, crayon, pencil, eraser.

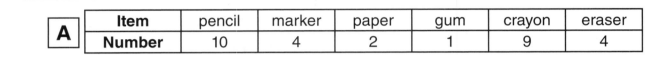

A

Item	pencil	marker	paper	gum	crayon	eraser
Number	10	4	2	1	9	4

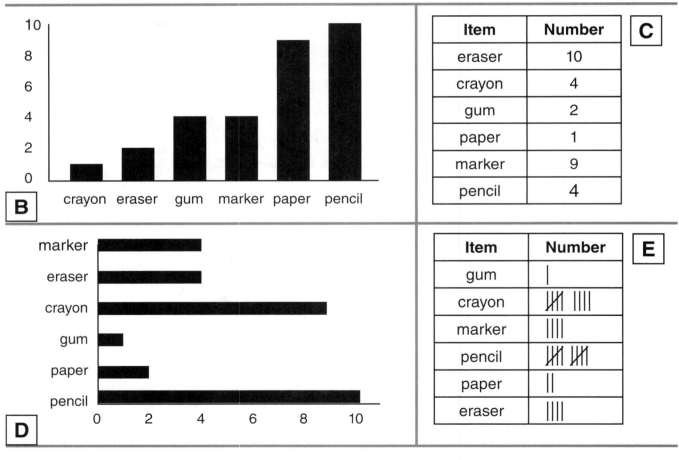

C

Item	Number
eraser	10
crayon	4
gum	2
paper	1
marker	9
pencil	4

E

Item	Number
gum	I
crayon	ЖН IIII
marker	IIII
pencil	ЖН ЖН
paper	II
eraser	IIII

F

Item	marker	gum	pencil	crayon	eraser	paper
Number	IIII	I	ЖН	ЖН IIII	IIII	ЖН

Graphs, Charts, and Diagrams

Skill 4: The student will represent, compare, and interpret a pictograph, a bar graph, a tally chart, a circle graph, and a Venn diagram.

Instructional Preparation

Materials:
- butcher paper
- set of markers (3 or 4) for each group

Duplicate the following (one per student, unless otherwise indicated):
- "Graphs, Charts, and Diagrams" reference sheet
- "What Does It Show?" worksheet

Prepare an overhead transparency of the following:
- "Graphs, Charts, and Diagrams" reference sheet
- "What Does It Show?" worksheet

Recall

Before beginning the **Review** component, facilitate a discussion based on these questions:

❋ What is a graph? (*a drawing that shows information in an organized way*)

❋ What different kinds of graphs are there? (*bar graphs, pictographs, circle graphs*)

❋ Can you think of any other ways we can show information? Any charts or diagrams? (*tally charts, Venn diagrams, etc.*)

Review

1. Ask the students who have only brothers to stand up. On the board write "Students with Only Brothers," and underneath that heading write the number of students who are standing. Have these students sit and then ask the students who have only sisters to stand. Write this number under the heading "Students with Only Sisters." Have these students sit and ask students who have both brothers and sisters to stand. Write this number on the board under the heading "Students with Both Brothers and Sisters." Have these students sit and now ask students who do not have any brothers or sisters to stand. Write this number on the board under the heading "Students with No Brothers or Sisters." Explain that today they are going to use this data to create several different types of graphs.

2. Distribute the "Graphs, Charts, and Diagrams" reference sheet and display the transparency. Ask for a volunteer to read the definition for "bar graph" from the "Words to Know" section. Direct the students' attention to the bar graph at the top of the page. Review with the class the different parts of a bar graph by asking the following questions:

❋ What is the title of this graph? (*"Trees at the Park"*)
❋ What are the labels on this graph? (*"Kind of Tree" and "Number of Trees"*)
❋ What information is this graph showing? (*the number of different trees at the park*)

Graphs, Charts, and Diagrams (*cont.*)

Review (*cont.*)

Point to the scale on the graph. Remind them that scales can show different increments. Ask the following question:

✳ What increments are on the scale? (*The scale goes up by 2s.*)

Point to the bars on the graph. Remind them to follow the bar to the end. This will tell them the value of the bar. Have the students look at the bar that represents the number of oak trees. Ask the following question:

✳ How many oak trees are at the park? (*14*)

Have the class look at the bar representing the number of aspens. Tell the class that this bar is between the numbers 16 and 18, so there are 17 aspens at the park. Ask the following questions:

✳ How many pine trees are there? (*11*)

✳ How can you find out how many more oak trees there are than pine trees? (*by subtracting the number of oaks from the number of pines, 14−11*)

✳ How can you find out the total number of trees there are at the park? (*by adding 14 + 17 + 11*)

✳ How many trees are there at the park? (*42*)

Remind the class that a bar graph can be shown with horizontal bars, like this one, or with vertical bars. The information does not change. If necessary, create a vertical bar graph on the board using the same data.

3. Have a volunteer read the definition of a circle graph. Then direct the students' attention to the circle graph. Ask the following question:

   ✳ What is the title of this graph? (*"Time Spent on Chores"*)

   Show the class the different parts of this graph, doing dishes, making the bed, emptying trash, and folding clothes. Tell the students that the larger the section, the more time that is spent on that chore. Ask the following questions:

   ✳ Which chore takes the longest amount of time? (*doing the dishes*)

   ✳ Which chores take the same amount of time? (*making the bed and emptying the trash*)

   ✳ Which chores together take the same amount of time as doing the dishes? (*making the bed, emptying the trash, and folding clothes*)

4. Have a different volunteer read the definition of a pictograph. Direct the students' attention to the pictograph. Give the students time to study this graph and then ask these questions:

   ✳ What is the title of this pictograph? (*"Favorite Activities"*)

   ✳ What are the labels on this graph? (*"Activity" and "Number of Votes"*)

   ✳ What are the different activities in this graph? (*board games, riding bikes, and reading*)

   Now direct their attention to the bottom of the pictograph. Point out that each happy face is worth 2 votes. Ask for volunteers to tell the number of votes each activity received (*board games, 12; riding bikes, 9; reading, 10*).

Graphs, Charts, and Diagrams *(cont.)*

Review *(cont.)*

5. Ask for a volunteer to read the definition of a tally chart. Review the details of the tally chart with the class, asking questions similar to those asked for the other graphs. Follow this pattern with the Venn diagram, asking what each part of the diagram represents. Explain to the students that if a piece of data does not fit into one of the sections, it is placed outside the circles. Answer any questions that arise. Tell the class that they will be able to use their reference sheet for their activity.

6. Divide the class into groups of 3 or 4. Each group will receive a sheet of butcher paper and markers. Assign each group a bar graph, circle graph, pictograph, tally chart, or Venn diagram. If you have more than five groups, have one group do a horizontal bar graph and another group a vertical bar graph. Vertical and horizontal versions of the pictograph and the tally chart can also be made. Explain to the groups that they will be taking the information about the number of brothers and sisters from the board and making their graphs, charts, and diagrams. Remind the class that they will need to include a title and labels and to use their reference sheet for guidance. Ask some groups doing the bar graphs and pictographs to include a scale showing increments of one and other groups to use a scale showing increments of more than one.

   Have the groups first do their work on a sheet of paper. When they have finished, have them raise their hands for you to check their work before they draw it on the butcher paper. Circulate throughout the room, monitoring the students.

7. When the groups have finished, display their work around the room. Have the groups stand up, one at a time, and explain how they made their graph. Compare the information on the graphs that used the different scales. Ask the following questions:

   ✳ Is the information on the graphs different? *(no)*

   ✳ Would using one graph instead of another be better? *(Answers will vary. Example: Yes, it would be better to use a scale of 2 on the pictograph so that you don't have to include as many pictures.)*

   When the students have finished presenting their graphs, charts, and diagrams, have them return to their desks and put away their reference page.

8. Distribute the "What Does It Show?" worksheet. Read the directions with the class and have them work on this individually. When they have completed the worksheet, display the transparency and review their answers.

Wrap-Up

To conclude this lesson, have the students write responses using complete sentences to the following prompts in their math journal or on a sheet of notebook paper. Allow adequate time for task completion and then ask various students to share their responses with the class.

✳ Explain when it would be better to use a bar graph instead of a pictograph. *(Answers may vary. Example: A bar graph would be better to use if you are comparing many different items or if you are using large numbers.)*

✳ Explain when it would be better to use a tally chart than a circle graph. *(Answers may vary. Example: A tally chart would be better to use if you want to know exactly how many of an item there are.)*

✳ How are graphs used in everyday life? *(when taking a survey or analyzing information)*

Graphs, Charts, and Diagrams *(cont.)*
Reference Sheet

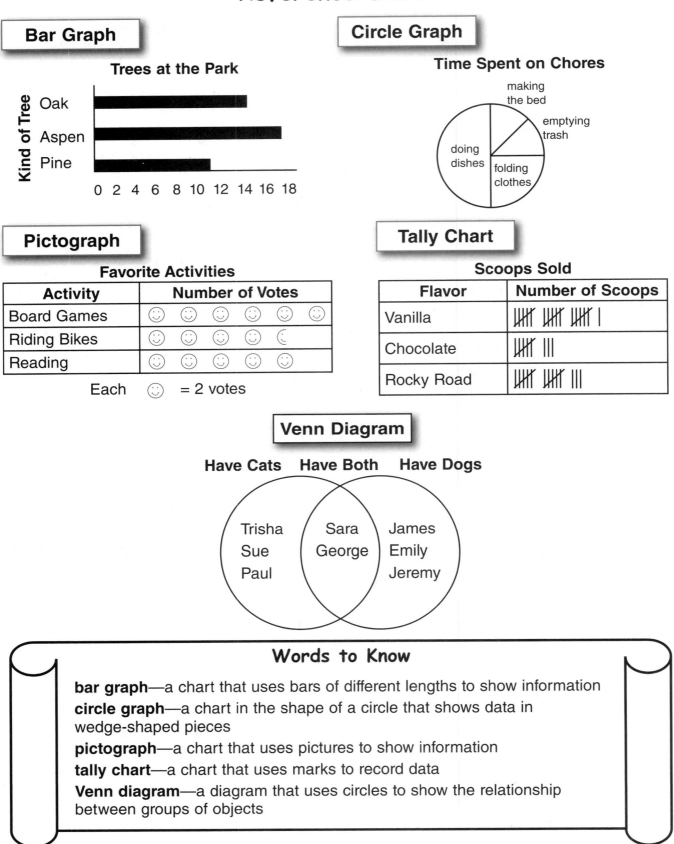

Bar Graph

Trees at the Park

Kind of Tree
Oak
Aspen
Pine

0 2 4 6 8 10 12 14 16 18

Circle Graph

Time Spent on Chores

making
the bed
emptying
trash
doing
dishes
folding
clothes

Pictograph

Favorite Activities

Activity	Number of Votes
Board Games	☺ ☺ ☺ ☺ ☺ ☺
Riding Bikes	☺ ☺ ☺ ☺ ☺
Reading	☺ ☺ ☺ ☺ ☺

Each ☺ = 2 votes

Tally Chart

Scoops Sold

Flavor	Number of Scoops
Vanilla	𝍩𝍩𝍩 𝍩𝍩𝍩 𝍩𝍩𝍩 I
Chocolate	𝍩𝍩𝍩 III
Rocky Road	𝍩𝍩𝍩 𝍩𝍩𝍩 III

Venn Diagram

Have Cats   Have Both   Have Dogs

Trisha
Sue
Paul

Sara
George

James
Emily
Jeremy

Words to Know

bar graph—a chart that uses bars of different lengths to show information

circle graph—a chart in the shape of a circle that shows data in wedge-shaped pieces

pictograph—a chart that uses pictures to show information

tally chart—a chart that uses marks to record data

Venn diagram—a diagram that uses circles to show the relationship between groups of objects

Name: _____

Graphs, Charts, and Diagrams *(cont.)*

What Does It Show?

Directions: Look at each graph, chart, and diagram. Answer the questions that follow each one.

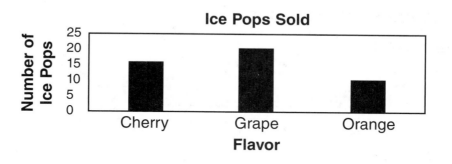

1. What is the title of this bar graph? _____
2. How many ice pops were sold in all? _____
3. What flavors of ice pops were sold? _____

Minutes Spent on Homework

Subject	Number of Minutes
Math	⦀⦀ ⦀⦀ ⦀⦀ ‖
Spelling	⦀⦀ ‖
Reading	⦀⦀ ⦀⦀ ⦀⦀
Science	⦀⦀ ⦀⦀ ‖‖

4. How much time was spent on homework in all? _____
5. What does the first column tell you? _____
6. How much more time was spent on reading homework than on spelling homework? _____

Animals We Saw

Kind	Number Seen
Zebra	x x
Giraffe	x
Monkey	x x x
Elephant	x

Each x = 3 animals.

7. What does each *x* represent? _____
8. How many zebras and elephants were seen? _____

Graphs, Charts, and Diagrams *(cont.)*

What Does It Show? *(cont.)*

Clothes in Tom's Chest

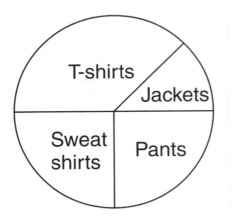

9. Which kind of clothing does Tom have the least of? _____

10. Which kind of clothing is there the most of in Tom's closet? _____

Favorite Sundae

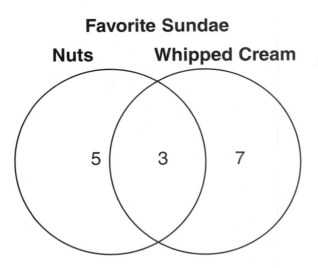

11. How many people like only nuts or whipped cream on their sundaes? _____

12. How many people like both nuts and whipped cream on their sundaes? _____

Congruence and Symmetry

Skill 5: The student will apply basic knowledge of congruence and symmetry.

Instructional Preparation

Materials:

- two different-sized equilateral or isosceles triangles (large enough for the class to see)

Duplicate the following (one per student, unless otherwise indicated):

- "How Do You Know?" reference sheet
- "Congruence and Symmetry" worksheet (*one per student pair*)
- "Circle It, Draw It, Write It" worksheet

Prepare an overhead transparency of the following:

- "How Do You Know?" reference sheet
- "Congruence and Symmetry" worksheet
- "Circle It, Draw It, Write It" worksheet

Recall

Before beginning the **Review** component, facilitate a discussion based on these questions:

- ✳ What objects in the classroom are the same shape?
- ✳ What objects in the classroom are the same shape and the same size?

Review

1. Hold up the two triangles. Ask the following questions:
   - ✳ How are these shapes the same? (*They are both triangles; they both have three vertices and three sides.*)
   - ✳ How are these shapes different? (*They are different sizes.*)

   Hold up just one of the triangles. Ask the following question:
   - ✳ How can this shape be divided into two equal parts? (*by drawing a line down the center*)

   Explain to the class that today they will be studying congruency and symmetry.

2. Distribute the "How Do You Know?" reference sheet and display the transparency. Review the terms and definitions in the "Words to Know" section with the class.

3. Direct attention to the top of the page. Have the class look at the first set of shapes.
   - ✳ Are these shapes congruent? (*no*)
   - ✳ How do you know? (*They are the same shape but not the same size.*)

   Have the class look at the second set of shapes.
   - ✳ Are these shapes congruent? (*yes*)
   - ✳ How do you know? (*They are the same shape and size.*)

   Point out that even though the shapes are not facing the same direction, they are still congruent. Circle these shapes on the transparency and have the students circle them on their papers. Now direct their attention to the last set of shapes and ask these questions:
   - ✳ Are these shapes congruent? (no)
   - ✳ How do you know? (They are the same size but not the same shape.)

Congruence and Symmetry *(cont.)*

Review *(cont.)*

4. Read the information in the second section with the students. Ask for a volunteer to give the definition of symmetry. Then direct attention to the heart. Ask these questions:

   ✳ Does the heart have a line of symmetry drawn through it? *(no)*
   ✳ How do you know? *(because both halves are not the same, or matching)*
   ✳ Is there a different place the line could be drawn to show a line of symmetry? *(yes, vertically down the center)*

   Follow this line of questioning with each of the other three shapes in this section, circling the moon, since it does show a line of symmetry.

5. Move to the third section. Explain to the class that they will be drawing a line of symmetry on whichever shape(s) they can. Give the class a few moments to decide on which shapes a line of symmetry can be drawn and to draw their lines. Then ask:

   ✳ Can a line of symmetry be drawn on the happy face? *(yes)*
   ✳ Where does the line need to be drawn? *(down the center)*
   ✳ Can another line of symmetry be drawn on the happy face? *(no)*

   Draw a line of symmetry down the center of the happy face and ask these questions:

   ✳ Can a line of symmetry be drawn on the arrow? *(no)* on the starburst? *(no)*
   ✳ Can a line of symmetry be drawn on the fourth shape? *(yes)*
   ✳ How does the line need to be drawn? *(horizontally)*
   ✳ Can another line of symmetry be drawn on this shape? *(no)*

6. Place the students in pairs and give each pair a "Congruence and Symmetry" worksheet. Read the first set of directions with the students. Have the pairs do this section. When they are finished, display the transparency and ask for volunteers to come to the overhead and circle the shapes they chose.

   Read the directions for the next section with the class. Have the pairs decide which shapes show a line of symmetry and have them write the numbers of the shapes on the line. When they have finished, ask them to give their answers. *(Answers: Shapes 1, 2, and 6 have lines of symmetry. Shapes 3, 4, and 5 do not.)*

   Answer any questions the class may have and then focus their attention on the last set of directions. Explain that some of the shapes do not have a line of symmetry, some have one, and some have more than one. Circulate the room to monitor the students as they work. When they have finished, ask them to share their answers on the transparency.

7. Distribute the "Circle It, Draw It, Write It" worksheet. Tell the students that they will be doing this page on their own. Circulate the room as the class works. When the students have finished, display the transparency and ask for volunteers to share their answers.

Wrap-Up

To conclude this lesson, have the students write responses using complete sentences to the following prompts in their math journal or on a sheet of notebook paper. Allow adequate time for task completion and then ask various students to share their responses with the class.

   ✳ What is congruency? *(figures having the same size and shape)*
   ✳ What is symmetry? *(a figure with matching halves)*
   ✳ When do you think you will use these skills in everyday life? *(Answers will vary.)*

Congruence and Symmetry *(cont.)*

How Do You Know?

Section 1: Look at each set of shapes. Which sets of shapes are congruent? How do you know?

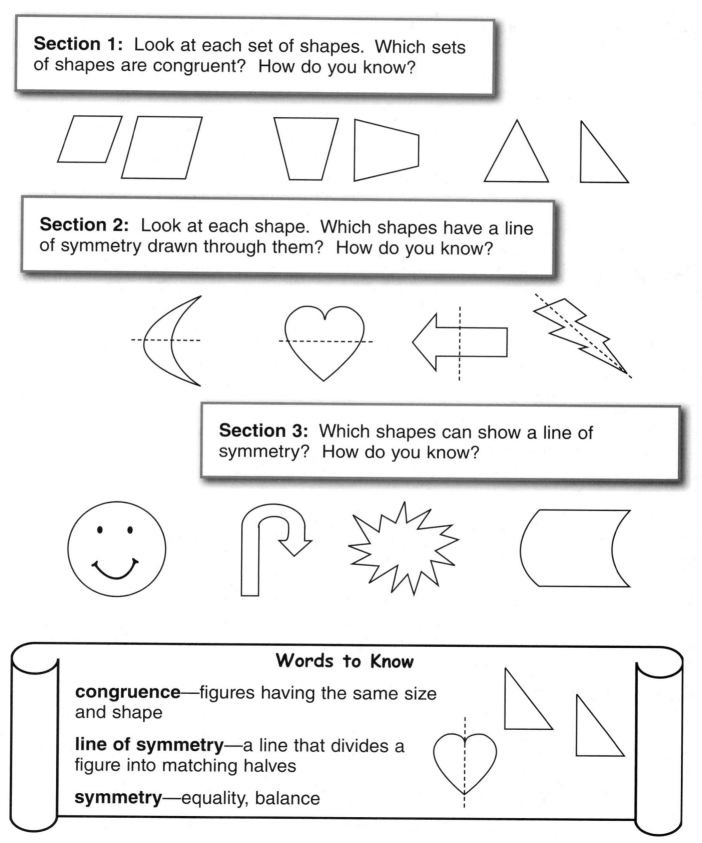

Section 2: Look at each shape. Which shapes have a line of symmetry drawn through them? How do you know?

Section 3: Which shapes can show a line of symmetry? How do you know?

Words to Know

congruence—figures having the same size and shape

line of symmetry—a line that divides a figure into matching halves

symmetry—equality, balance

Congruence and Symmetry *(cont.)*

Congruence and Symmetry

Directions: Circle the shapes that are congruent in each set.

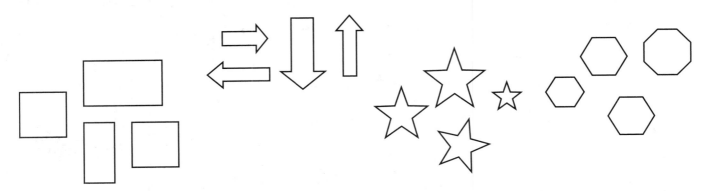

Directions: Write down the numbers of the shapes that show a line of symmetry.

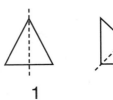 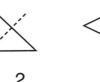 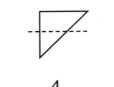 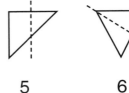

These shapes show a line of symmetry: _____

Directions: Draw a line of symmetry through each shape that you can. Be careful, as some shapes have more than one line of symmetry!

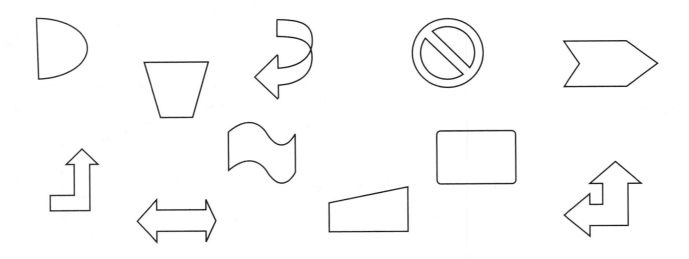

Name: _____

Congruence and Symmetry *(cont.)*
Circle It, Draw It, Write It

1. Circle the shapes that are congruent.

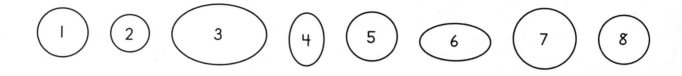

2. Draw one line of symmetry through each of the following shapes.

3. What is congruence?

_____

_____

_____

4. What is a symmetrical figure?

_____

_____

_____

Two- and Three-Dimensional Shapes

Skill 6: The student will describe, classify, and sort two- and three-dimensional shapes according to their attributes.

Instructional Preparation

Materials:

- large picture of a ball
- actual ball

Duplicate the following (one per student, unless otherwise indicated):

- "Figures" reference sheet
- "Which Figure Am I?" worksheet (one per group)
- "I Know My Figures!" worksheet

Prepare an overhead transparency of the following:

- "Figures" reference sheet
- "Which Figure Am I?" worksheet
- "I Know My Figures!" worksheet

Recall

Before beginning the **Review** component, facilitate a discussion based on the following questions:

 ✳ What is the difference between two-dimensional and three-dimensional figures? (*Answers will vary and may include that two-dimensional figures are flat and three-dimensional figures take up space.*)

 ✳ How can you describe different figures? (*Answers will vary and may include counting the number of sides, faces, edges, and vertices.*)

Review

1. Show the class a picture of a ball. Then hold up a real ball. Ask the students what the difference is between the picture and the actual ball. (*Answers will vary and may include that the picture is flat and the ball takes up space.*) Explain to the class that today they will be studying two- and three-dimensional figures and how they can be described.

2. Distribute the "Figures" reference sheet and display the transparency. Direct the students' attention to the "Words to Know" section at the bottom of the page. Review the terms and definitions for two-dimensional figures with the students.

Two- and Three-
Dimensional Shapes *(cont.)*

Review *(cont.)*

3. Have the students look at the figures in the first section of the reference sheet. Ask for a volunteer to say the name of each shape as you point to it on the overhead. Explain to the class that even though each figure has a specific name, the figures can also be described using the number of sides and vertices they have. Ask these questions:

   ✳ How many sides are on the square? *(4)*

   ✳ How many vertices are on the square? *(4)*

   ✳ How many sides are on the circle? *(none—a circle does not have any line segments)*

   ✳ How many vertices are on the circle? *(none)*

   Continue this line of questioning for the other figures in this section. Explain that one way to sort plane figures is by the number of sides and vertices they have. Ask:

   ✳ Which two figures would be sorted together based on their having the same number of sides and vertices? *(the square and the rhombus)*

   ✳ How do you know? *(They each have 4 sides and 4 vertices.)*

   ✳ What figures in this room are two-dimensional? *(sheets of paper, posters on the wall, etc.)*

4. Ask a volunteer to read the terms and definitions for three-dimensional figures in the "Words to Know" section. Hold up the picture of the ball and the actual ball. Ask the students in which categories the picture of the ball and the actual ball belong. *(The picture of the ball is two-dimensional; the actual ball is three-dimensional.)*

5. Direct the students' attention to the second section on the reference sheet. Ask for a volunteer to name each shape as you point to it on the overhead. Explain to the students that, just as the two-dimensional figures can be described by the number of vertices and sides they have, these figures can be described using the number of edges, faces, and vertices they have. Ask the following questions:

   ✳ How many edges are on a cube? *(12)*

   ✳ How many faces are on a cube? *(6)*

   ✳ What kinds of faces are on a cube? *(They are all squares.)*

   ✳ How many vertices are on a cube? *(8)*

   ✳ How many faces are on a cylinder? *(2)*

   Explain to the class that there are two round faces on a cylinder and one curved surface. Point out that the cone has one round base and one curved surface. Ask how a sphere can be described *(as having one curved surface)*. Ask the following questions:

   ✳ Which two figures would be sorted together based on having the same number of edges, faces, and vertices? *(the cube and the rectangular prism)*

   ✳ How are the cube and the rectangular prism different? *(On the cube, all the faces are squares; on the rectangular prism, all the faces are rectangles.)*

   ✳ What objects in this room are three-dimensional figures? *(Answers may vary.)*

Two- and Three-Dimensional Shapes *(cont.)*

Review *(cont.)*

6. Divide the class into groups of two or three. Give each group a copy of the "Which Figure Am I?" worksheet and display the transparency. Have each member of the group write his or her name on the line that says "Figure Makers' Names." Read the directions with the class. Make sure all the groups have their reference sheets out while they are writing the numbers of sides and vertices (or edges, faces, and vertices) that a figure has. When the groups finish, collect the worksheets and have the students put away their reference sheets. Display the "Figures" reference sheet on the overhead, covering up the "Words to Know" section. Tell the students that now they will be solving one another's worksheets.

   Distribute the collected worksheets to different groups. Have each member of the group write his or her name on the line that says "Figure Solvers' Names." Next, the students determine which shapes have been described and then write the names of the shapes on the "Which figure am I?" line. When the groups have finished, allow the students to use their reference sheets to check their group's answers and then return the worksheets to the students whose names are on the "Figure Makers' Names" line. Ask the following questions:

   ✳ Which terms are used to describe a two-dimensional figure? (*"side" and "vertex"*)

   ✳ Which terms are used to describe a three-dimensional figure? (*"edge," "face," and "vertex"*)

   Answer any questions that the students may have, collect the worksheets, and have the students return to their desks.

7. Distribute the "I Know My Figures!" worksheet and display the transparency. Read each set of directions with the class. Have the students work on this independently. When all the students have finished, ask for volunteers to share their answers and write them on the transparency.

Wrap-Up

To conclude this lesson, have the students write responses using complete sentences to the following prompts in their math journal or on a sheet of notebook paper. Allow adequate time for task completion and then ask various students to share their responses with the class.

   ✳ Explain the difference between two-dimensional and three-dimensional figures. (*Two-dimensional figures are flat; they have only length and width. Three-dimensional figures take up more space; they have length, width, and depth.*)

   ✳ How can two-dimensional figures be described? (*by the number of sides and vertices*)

   ✳ How can three-dimensional figures be described? (*by the number of edges, faces, and vertices*)

   ✳ Give some examples of two-dimensional and three-dimensional figures found in real life.

Two- and Three-Dimensional Shapes *(cont.)*

2-D (Two-dimensional) Figures

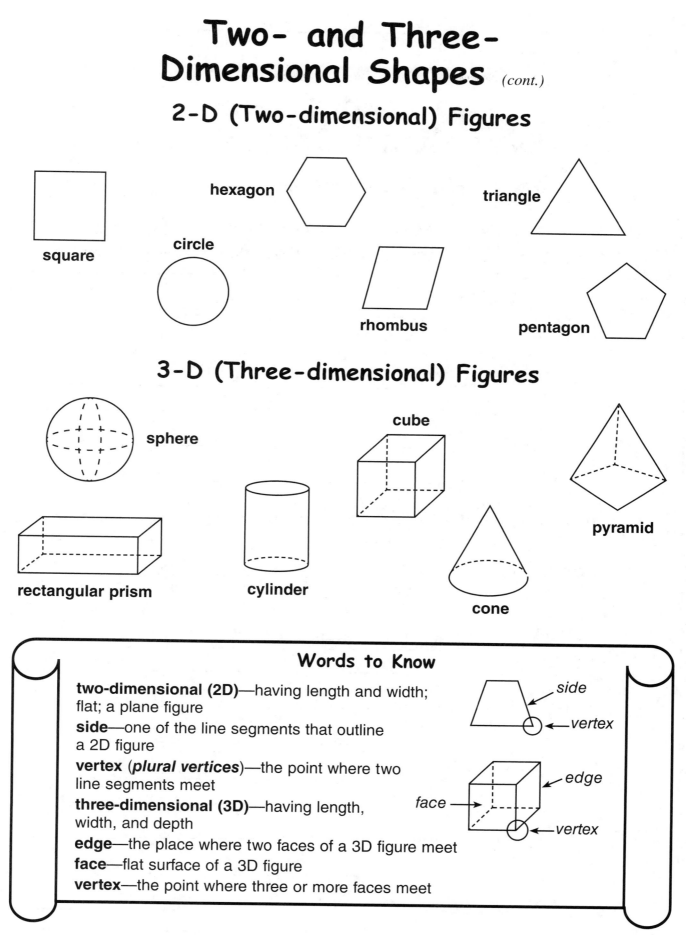

square

hexagon

triangle

circle

rhombus

pentagon

3-D (Three-dimensional) Figures

sphere

cube

rectangular prism

cylinder

cone

pyramid

Words to Know

two-dimensional (2D)—having length and width; flat; a plane figure

side—one of the line segments that outline a 2D figure

vertex (*plural vertices*)—the point where two line segments meet

three-dimensional (3D)—having length, width, and depth

edge—the place where two faces of a 3D figure meet

face—flat surface of a 3D figure

vertex—the point where three or more faces meet

side

vertex

edge

face

vertex

Figure Makers' Names: _____

Figure Solvers' Names: _____

Two- and Three- Dimensional Shapes *(cont.)*

Which Figure Am I?

Directions: Describe two-dimensional and three-dimensional figures using the terms on your "Figures" reference sheet (page 37). Double-check your work!

1. I am a figure with _____

_____

Which figure am I? _____

2. I am a figure with _____

_____

Which figure am I? _____

3. I am a figure with _____

_____

Which figure am I? _____

4. I am a figure with _____

_____

Which figure am I? _____

5. I am a figure with _____

_____

Which figure am I? _____

Two- and Three-Dimensional Shapes (cont.)

I Know My Figures!

Directions: Write the parts of each figure on the lines.

1.

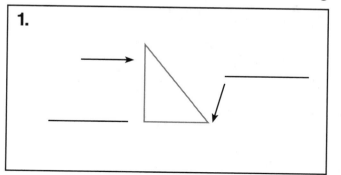

2.

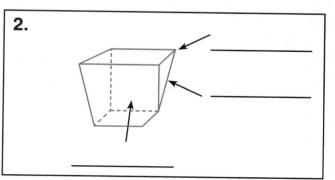

Directions: Describe each figure below.

- Circle 2-D or 3-D.

- Describe each figure by its number of vertices and sides (or vertices, faces, and edges). Your answer should include the number and the term.

3.   **4.**   **5.**   **6.**

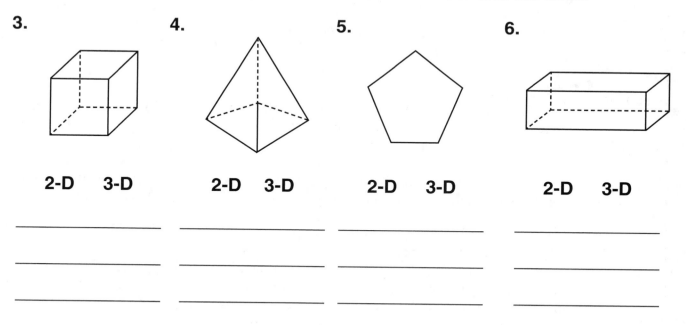

2-D   3-D   2-D   3-D   2-D   3-D   2-D   3-D

Units of Measure

Skill 7: The student will apply the concept of appropriate units when measuring weight, length, and capacity.

Instructional Preparation

Duplicate the following (one per student, unless otherwise indicated):

- "Table of Measures" reference sheet
- "Which Unit Is It?" worksheet (*one per student pair*)
- "Choose the Unit" worksheet

Prepare an overhead transparency of the following:

- "Table of Measures" reference sheet
- "Which Unit Is It?" worksheet
- "Choose the Unit" worksheet

Recall

Before beginning the **Review** component, facilitate a discussion based on the following questions:

✶ What can you do to find out how tall you are? (*measure your height*)

✶ What can be used to measure your height? (*Answers will vary and may include the following: a measuring bar attached to a scale at a doctor's office, a tape measure, or a yardstick.*)

Review

1. Tell the class that you want to know how much your favorite book weighs. Take out your ruler and measure the length of your book. Tell them the number of inches your book weighs. Ask what is wrong with the measurement you just used. After they have answered that weight is not measured in inches, have a discussion about using correct units. Explain that it is important to use correct units when measuring length, weight, and capacity. Tell them that today they will be studying these different units.

2. Distribute the "Table of Measures" reference sheet and display the metric transparency. Review the terms and definitions in the "Words to Know" section at the bottom of the second page with the students. Explain that the metric system is used around the world. Tell them that many people in the United States use the metric system in their work, so it is important for the students to be familiar with it. As an example, mention that the doses of most medicine are given in metric amounts.

Review *(cont.)*

3. Display the first page of the "Table of Measures" transparency and review each of the U.S. customary measurements with the class. Explain that using familiar objects as a benchmark for a unit can help. It's easier when you can compare what you are measuring to something you already know. Encourage them to come up with another example for each unit given. Then ask the following questions:

   ✳ To find the length of your bike, would you use feet or miles? (*feet*)

   ✳ Why? (*Answers may vary but should include that a mile is a very long distance.*)

   ✳ At the grocery store, do you measure a bag of potatoes in ounces or pounds? (*pounds*)

   ✳ How do you know? (*Answers will vary and may include that potatoes are heavy, and many times are sold in 5- or 10-pound bags.*)

4. Display the second page of the "Table of Measures" transparency and review each of the metric measurements with the class. Encourage them to come up with other examples for each unit given; for example, a centimeter is also about the width of a fingernail.

5. Place the students in pairs. Distribute the first page of the "Which Unit Is It?" worksheet and display the transparency. Read the directions with them. Circulate throughout the room to monitor student progress. When they have finished, have them take out their reference pages to check their work. Then review the answers together as a class.

   Now have them put away their reference sheets, and distribute the second page of the worksheet. Read these directions to the class. Explain that the number of units they choose needs to be realistic. When the pairs have finished, display the "Table of Measures" transparency and ask for volunteers to share their answers. Have the students return to their seats.

6. Distribute the "Choose the Unit" worksheet and display the transparency. Read the directions with the class. They will work on this individually. When finished, review the answers as a class.

Wrap-Up

To conclude this lesson, have the students write responses using complete sentences to the following prompts in their math journal or on a sheet of notebook paper. Allow adequate time for task completion and then ask various students to share their responses with the class.

   ✳ What units are used to measure length? (*U.S. customary units: inch, foot, yard, mile; metric units: centimeter, meter, kilometer*)

   ✳ What units are used to measure weight? (*U.S. customary units: ounce and pound; metric units: gram and kilogram*)

   ✳ What units are used to measure capacity? (*U.S. customary units: cup, gallon, pint, quart; metric units: milliliter and liter*)

   ✳ Why is it important to know the different units used in measuring? (*Answers will vary.*)

Units of Measure *(cont.)*

Table of Measures

Customary Units

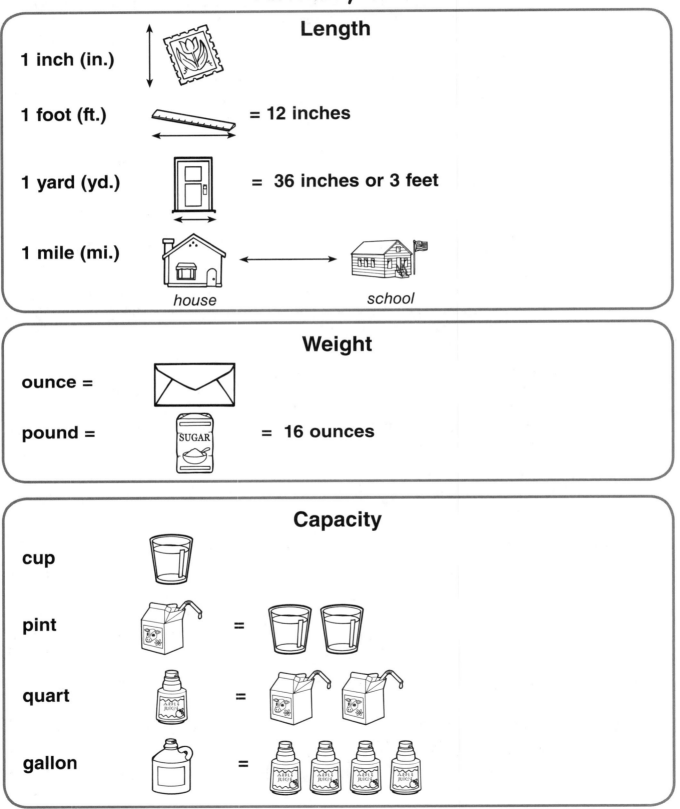

Length

1 inch (in.)

1 foot (ft.) = 12 inches

1 yard (yd.) = 36 inches or 3 feet

1 mile (mi.)

house   *school*

Weight

ounce =

pound = = 16 ounces

Capacity

cup

pint =

quart =

gallon =

Units of Measure *(cont.)*

Table of Measures *(cont.)*

Metric Units

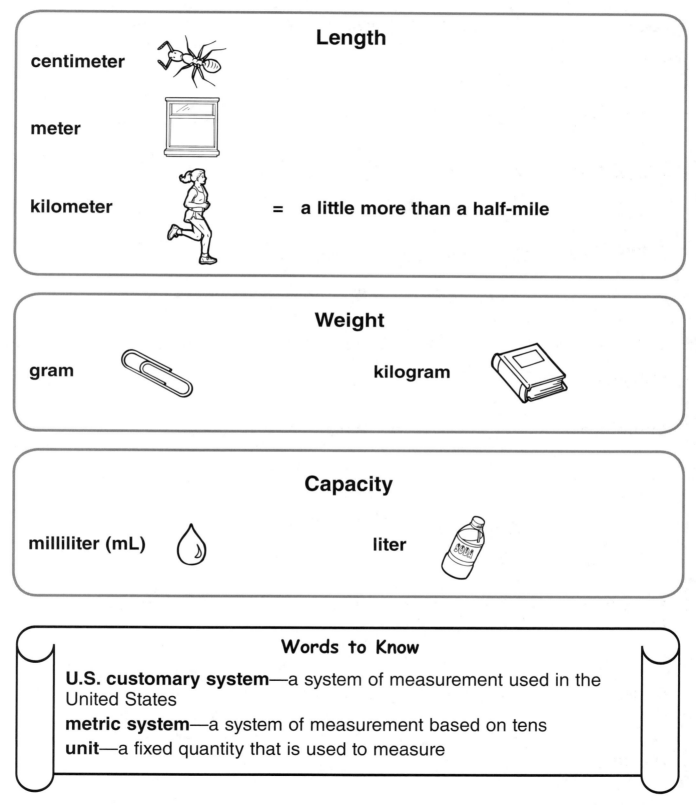

Length

centimeter

meter

kilometer = **a little more than a half-mile**

Weight

gram

kilogram

Capacity

milliliter (mL)

liter

Words to Know

U.S. customary system—a system of measurement used in the United States

metric system—a system of measurement based on tens

unit—a fixed quantity that is used to measure

Units of Measure *(cont.)*
Which Unit Is It?

Directions: Read each question. Circle the measurement that uses the correct unit(s).

1. About how much water will fill a bathtub?

20 cups   20 gallons   20 ounces

2. About how far could it be from one side of a city to the other?

15 centimeters   15 feet   15 miles

3. What is most likely the weight of a bicycle?

15 pounds   15 yards   15 ounces

4. About how much medicine will a baby receive?

3 milliliters   3 liters   3 cups

5. Ten people are going to a party. About how much punch will be needed?

5 meters   5 milliliters   5 liters

6. What is most likely the distance John walked in 30 minutes?

3 centimeters   3 kilometers   3 meters

7. Carla bought 20 apples. What is most likely the weight of the apples?

3 liters   3 grams   3 kilograms

8. About how much does a third-grader weigh?

50 pounds   50 ounces   50 gallons

Units of Measure *(cont.)*

Which Unit Is It?

Directions: Read each question. Draw a line from the graphic to the unit that should be used to measure it. Then write an approximate measurement that would be reasonable on the line.

9. About how long is a grasshopper?

_____ centimeters

_____ meters

10. About how long is a pencil?

_____ inches

_____ yards

11. What is most likely the amount of juice Sam drank with breakfast?

_____ cup(s)

_____ quart(s)

12. About how much do four feathers weigh?

_____ grams

_____ kilograms

13. Johnny has a new slide. What is most likely the height of his slide?

_____ miles

_____ feet

Units of Measure (cont.)

Choose the Unit

Directions: Circle the reasonable measurement.

1. About how tall is a flower?

        8 yards   8 ounces   8 inches

2. About how much does a bowling ball weigh?

        12 ounces   12 pounds   12 gallons

3. About how much does a slice of toast weigh?

        1 ounce   1 kilogram   1 centimeter

4. About how much sugar would you put in a cake?

        2 quarts   2 cups   2 yards

5. About how long is the parking lot at school?

        40 kilometers   40 centimeters   40 meters

6. What is most likely the weight of a straw?

        2 inches   2 grams   2 milliliters

7. What is most likely the amount of eye drops Chrissy placed in her eye?

        4 milliliters   4 liters   4 grams

8. About how long is a skateboard?

        2 pounds   2 yards   2 feet

Measurement Tools

Skill 8: The student will choose and apply the appropriate measurement tool for a given situation.

Instructional Preparation

Duplicate the following (one per student, unless otherwise indicated):

- "How We Measure" reference sheet
- "Which Tool Should Be Used?" worksheet (one per student pair)
- "Choose the Measurement Tool" worksheet

Prepare an overhead transparency of the following:

- "How We Measure" reference sheet
- "Choose the Measurement Tool" worksheet

Recall

Before beginning the **Review** component, facilitate a discussion based on the following questions:

✳ What are some objects that we can measure? (*Answers will vary.*)

✳ Why is it important to be able to measure different things? (*Answers will vary.*)

Review

1. Ask 10 students to line up in the front of the room. Without explaining why, start placing them in order according to height. Ask the rest of the class if they can see how you arranged the students. Explain that measuring height involves one of the measuring tools that we use. To find out the height of each of these students, we could use a measuring tape. Have the volunteers return to their desks and explain that today the students are going to decide which measurement tool to use to solve a given problem.

2. Distribute the "How We Measure" reference sheet and display the transparency. Review the terms and definitions in the "Words to Know" section with the class.

3. Direct attention to the information at the top of the page about time. Read the first section with the class. After reading the questions that can be answered using clocks, ask the following questions:

✳ When have we used a clock in school to measure time? (*Answers will vary.*)

✳ What is another situation when you would use a clock to measure time? (*Answers will vary.*)

Measurement Tools (cont.)

Review (cont.)

Read the section on calendars with the class. Ask the following questions:

 ✳ When have we used a calendar in class to measure time? (*Answers will vary.*)

 ✳ What is another situation when you would use a calendar to measure time? (*Answers will vary.*)

Continue using the method above for the remaining sections on the reference sheet. First, read through the section, then ask for additional situations when each of the measurement tools can be used.

4. Place the students in pairs. Distribute the "Which Tool Should Be Used?" worksheet. Read the directions with them. Tell them that they may use their reference sheet for guidance; however, the situations they write need to be different from the ones on the reference sheet and the ones discussed in class. Circulate around the room to monitor the students as they write their situations. When the pairs are finished, have them exchange them with another pair. Now they need to decide which measurement tool could be used to solve the problem. Have them write down their answers on the lines. When finished, have the pairs get together to discuss the situations and their answers. Ask for volunteers to share some of the situations they wrote. Have the students return to their seats.

5. Distribute the "Choose the Measurement Tool" worksheet. Read the directions with the class and have them work on this individually. When they have completed the worksheet, display the transparency and review their answers.

Wrap-Up

To conclude this lesson, have the students write responses using complete sentences to the following prompts in their math journal or on a sheet of notebook paper. Allow adequate time for task completion and then ask various students to share their responses with the class.

 ✳ What are some measuring tools? (*clocks; calendars; measuring cups; containers used to hold pints, quarts, and gallons; rulers; yardsticks; tape measures; scales; and thermometers.*)

 ✳ What do we use them for? (*telling time; finding dates; and measuring capacity, length, width, height, weight, and temperature.*)

 ✳ When do we use measuring tools in day-to-day life? (*Answers will vary.*)

Measurement Tools *(cont.)*

How We Measure

Time

We use *clocks* to measure time.
- How many minutes did you play basketball?
- What time will it be in 30 minutes?

We also use *calendars* to measure time.
- How many days until your grandmother is visiting?
- How many months until your birthday?

Capacity

Measuring cups and *pint, quart,* and *gallon* containers are used as tools in measuring capacity. They tell us how much liquid (such as water) or solid (such as sand) an object holds.

Length, Width/Height

Rulers, yardsticks, and *tape measures* are used to find length, width, and height.
- How tall are you?
- How long is my bike?

Scales are used to measure weight. We can use a scale to find out the weight of a new puppy or even to find the weight of 6 apples at the store.

Weight

Temperature

A *thermometer* is used to tell the temperature. The higher the temperature, the warmer it is.
- Should I wear a sweater today?

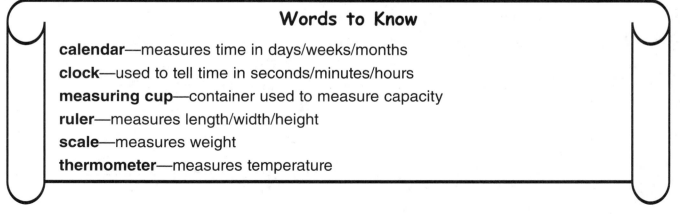

Words to Know

calendar—measures time in days/weeks/months

clock—used to tell time in seconds/minutes/hours

measuring cup—container used to measure capacity

ruler—measures length/width/height

scale—measures weight

thermometer—measures temperature

Measurement Tools *(cont.)*

Which Tool Should Be Used?

Directions: Write four different situations that each would each require a different measurement tool. Do not write the tool that will be used—save that for the next pair of students to figure out.

1.

_____

_____

_____

Measurement tool: _____

2.

_____

_____

_____

Measurement tool: _____

3.

_____

_____

_____

Measurement tool: _____

4.

_____

_____

_____

Measurement tool: _____

Measurement Tools (cont.)

Choose the Measurement Tool

Directions: Read each situation. Choose the best measurement tool to use from the box. Write your answer on the line. (Each measurement tool may be used more than once.)

clock	calendar	thermometer
scale	tape measure	measuring cup
gallon container		

1. Which measurement tool is used to measure the length of a stick?

   _____

2. Which measurement tool should Mandy use to find out how many minutes she was reading? _____

3. Which measurement tool will show Phil if he should wear a jacket?

   _____

4. Which measurement tool would be best to use to find out the amount of water it will take to fill the bathtub?

   _____

5. Which measurement tool should Jeremy use to find out the weight of his boot?

   _____

6. Which measurement tool shows the number of weeks until Valentine's Day?

   _____

7. Which measurement tool should Mom use to put the right amount of flour in the cake? _____

8. Which measurement tool will show you how long this worksheet is taking to finish? _____

Counting Money

Skill 9: The student will find and compare the value of a collection of pennies, nickels, dimes, quarters, and dollars.

Instructional Preparation

Materials:

- overhead coins and bills (*same increments and amounts as on the "Cutouts" reference sheet*)

Duplicate the following (one per student, unless otherwise indicated):

- "Counting Money" reference sheet
- "Cutouts" (*one per group, if needed to replace money listed above*) reference sheets
- "How Much?" worksheet

Prepare an overhead transparency of the following:

- "Counting Money" reference sheet
- "Money" reference sheet
- "How Much?" worksheet

Recall

Before beginning the **Review** component, facilitate a discussion based on the following questions:

※ What are bills and coins? (*dollars, various coins, etc.*)

※ When do you use money? (*Answers will vary.*)

※ Why is it important to be able to count money? (*Answers will vary.*)

Review

1. Hand a girl volunteer a new pencil and ask her to stand in the front of the room. Give a boy volunteer a handful of coins and have him also stand in the front of the room. Tell the girl she will be selling the pencil to the boy. Have the boy ask, "How much does your pencil cost? I would like to buy it." Have the girl give an amount. Tell the boy to give all of the coins to the girl to purchase the pencil. Ask the following questions:

※ What should the boy have done differently? (*He should have counted the money that was needed to buy the pencil.*)

※ Why? (*He may have given her too much or not enough money for the pencil.*)

Explain that today the class will be counting and comparing different amounts of money.

Counting Money *(cont.)*

Review *(cont.)*

2. Distribute the "Counting Money" reference sheet and display the transparency. Review the terms and definitions in the "Words to Know" section at the bottom of the page. Point out that coins can be shown with either heads or tails.

3. Direct the students' attention to the top of the page. Ask the following questions:

   ✳ What is the value of a penny? *(1¢)*

   ✳ What is the value of these pennies? *(7¢)*

   Write "7¢" next to the group of pennies. Have the students look at the section containing the nickels. Ask the students the value of a nickel *(5¢)*. Explain that skip counting is used in counting money. As a class, skip count by 5s to find the total value of these coins *(30¢)*. Write this amount next to the group of nickels. Follow this line of questioning for the sections containing dimes and quarters. Show the class that we can write the value of the quarters as 150¢. However, the usual way would be using the dollar sign *($1.50)*. Draw another quarter and skip count as a class to find the new value. Ask a student how to write this new amount using the dollar sign and write it on the transparency. *($1.75)*

4. Look at the last section of the "Counting Money" transparency and direct attention to the collection of coins. Have a volunteer read the information. As a class, count the value of these coins, going from the largest value to the smallest value *(67¢)*. To better explain why a collection of coins is counted using the largest coin first, count these coins as a class going from the smallest value to the largest value. Draw in a few extra coins, if needed, to emphasize this. Now draw in 1 five-dollar bill and 3 one-dollar bills. Tell the class that bills are added in the same way, the largest to the smallest value. Show how to write this new amount using the dollar sign *($8.67)*.

5. Place the students in groups of three and distribute sets of coins and bills or the "Cutouts" pages *(have them cut out the money on these pages)*. Display the "Money" transparency only showing the first problem. Have each group read number one and place this amount of money together and count it. Remind the students to count from the largest value to the smallest value. Ask for a volunteer to share his or her group's total with the class *(66¢)*. Check to see if the other groups have the same total. Place this number of coins on the overhead and count them as a class. Write the amount on the transparency *(66¢)*. Then show the students the second problem. Have them group these bills and coins and count them. Repeat this process with each problem on the "Money transparency" through #6. *(The answers are as follows: 2. $7.55; 3. $44.01; 4. $21.53; 5. $1.64; 6. $72.82.)*

Counting Money *(cont.)*

Review *(cont.)*

For number 7, have each group organize and count each set of money. Ask these questions:

✳ Which set of money has the highest value, set 1 or set 2? (*They both have the same value, $5.41.*)

✳ How can they have the same value when they each used different bills and a different amount of coins? (*four quarters has the same value as $1, etc.*)

For number 8, have each group organize and count each set of money. Ask the following questions:

✳ How much money is in each of the two sets? (*Set 1 has $1.26, and set 2 has $1.28.*)

✳ Which set has less money? (*Set 1 has less money, since they both have one dollar but 26¢ is less than 28¢.*)

Have them put all of the cutout money together. How much money do you have in all? (*$82.10*)

Collect the money and have the students go back to their seats.

6. Distribute the "How Much?" worksheet and display the transparency. Read the directions with the class. Mention that some questions will require them to circle their answer and some to write their answer on the lines, while others will ask for both. The students will complete the worksheet on their own. When the students are finished, ask for volunteers to write their answers on the transparency.

Wrap-Up

To conclude this lesson, have the students write a response using complete sentences to the following prompt in their math journal or on a sheet of notebook paper. Allow adequate time for task completion and then ask various students to share their responses with the class.

✳ When do you use money in your everyday life? (*when making a purchase*)

✳ Why is it important to be able to count money? (*to know if you have enough money to make a purchase at the store*)

✳ Why is it important to know how to compare different amounts of money? (*Answers will vary.*)

Counting Money *(cont.)*

Reference Sheet

To count a set of pennies, you count by 1s.

To count a set of dimes, you count by 10s.

To could a set of nickels, you count by 5s.

To count a set of quarters, you count by 25s.

To count a collection of different coins, you count the largest to the smallest values.

Words to Know

bill—a piece of money made of a rectangular piece of paper with a design on both sides

coin—a piece of money made of metal with a design on both sides

dime—a coin representing 10 cents

dollar—a bill representing 100 cents

nickel—a coin representing five cents

penny—a coin representing one cent

quarter—a coin representing 25 cents

Counting Money *(cont.)*

Cutouts

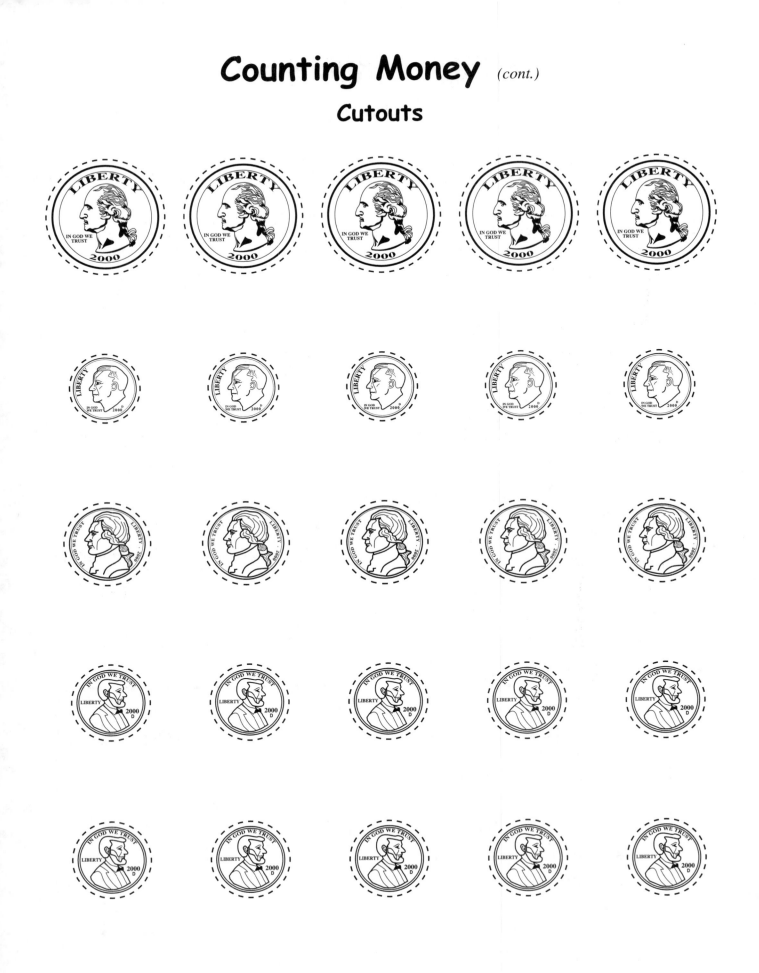

Counting Money *(cont.)*

Cutouts *(cont.)*

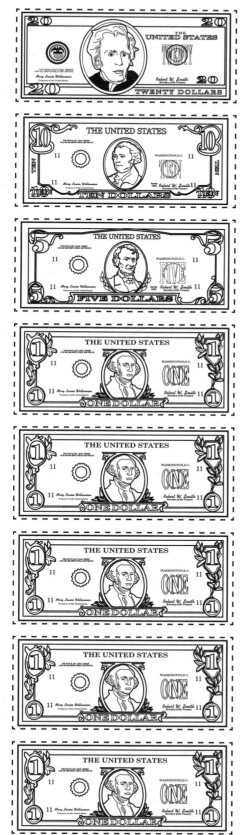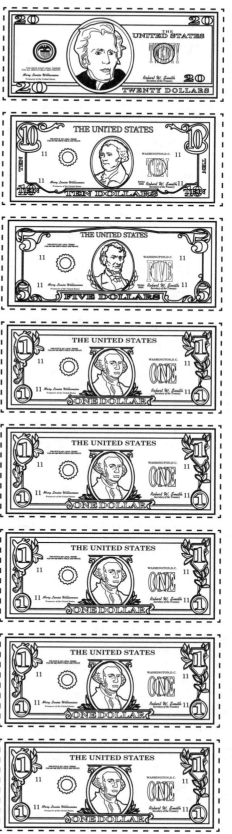

Counting Money *(cont.)*

Money

1. 1 quarter, 3 dimes, 1 nickel, 6 pennies

2. 1 five-dollar bill, 2 one-dollar bills, 4 dimes, 3 nickels

3. 2 twenty-dollar bills, 3 one-dollar bills, 2 quarters, 3 dimes, 4 nickels, 1 penny

4. 1 ten-dollar bill, 2 five-dollar bills, 1 one-dollar bill, 1 quarter, 1 dime, 2 nickels, 8 pennies.

5. 4 quarters, 3 dimes, 5 nickels, 9 pennies

6. 2 twenty-dollar bills, 2 ten-dollar bills, 2 five-dollar bills, 2 one-dollar bills, 2 quarters, 2 dimes, 2 nickels, 2 pennies

7.

Set 1	**Set 2**
4 one-dollar bills 1 penny 2 nickels 3 dimes 4 quarters	1 five-dollar bill 1 quarter 1 dime 1 nickel 1 penny

8.

Set 1	**Set 2**
1 penny 2 nickels 4 dimes 3 quarters	2 quarters 5 dimes 4 nickels 8 pennies

9. How much money do you have in all?

Name: _____

Counting Money *(cont.)*
How Much?

1. Sandra has the amount of money shown. How much money does she have?

Sandra has _____.

2. In the boxes below, write the amount of money Zack and Terri each have.
Circle the name of the person who has less money.

Zach   **Terri**

3. Jerry found this money in his pocket. How much money did Jerry find?

Jerry found _____.

Counting Money *(cont.)*

How Much? *(cont.)*

4. Write the amount of change Tony and Jan each have on the lines. Who received more change?

Tony   _____

Jan   _____

_____ received more change.

5. Circle the amount of money Adam has on his dresser.

$2.71

$2.81

$2.91

6. Betty, Kyle, and Juan each earned money this month doing chores. Write the amount earned next to each of their names. Who earned the most money?

_____

Time

Skill 10: The student will find the duration of intervals of time in hours.

Instructional Preparation

Materials:

- teacher Judy clock
- student Judy clocks

Duplicate the following (one per student, unless otherwise indicated):

- "How Much Time?" reference sheet
- "Find the Time" worksheet (*one per student pair*)
- "The Time Is . . ." worksheet

Prepare an overhead transparency of the following:

- "How Much Time?" reference sheet
- "Find the Time" worksheet
- "The Time Is . . ." worksheet

Recall

Before beginning the **Review** component, facilitate a discussion based on the following questions:

- ✳ What do we use a clock for? (*to tell time*)
- ✳ Why is it important to know the time? (*knowing when a television show or a baseball game will begin, etc.*)

Review

1. Ask a few students what they did last night. Choose one who did an activity and ask him or her what time the activity started and what time it ended. Write these times on the board. Explain that today the students are going to find elapsed time.

2. Distribute the "How Much Time?" reference sheet and display the transparency. Direct their attention to the "Words to Know" section at the bottom of the page. Review the terms and definitions as a class. Answer any questions the students may have.

3. Read the sentence in the top box. (*"What time do each of these clocks show?"*) Ask for volunteers to tell you the time. Write it on the line next to the clock. Have a different student read the information under each clock. Tell the class that this is something that could happen to them. Ask them what strategy they could use to find how much time Jeremy spent at his friend's house. If counting on is not mentioned, explain that for this example, counting on would be a good strategy. Use your Judy clock to show this by setting the clock to 3:00 and moving the hands to show one hour, 4:00, and two hours, 5:00.

Time *(cont.)*

Review *(cont.)*

4. Show 9:00 on the Judy clock. Tell the class that when you were growing up, you started school at 9:00 and got out at 3:00. *(These times show elapsed time in hours. Vary the times, if preferred.)* Ask the following question:

   ✳ What strategy can you use to find the number of hours you spent in school? *(start at 9:00 and count on)*

   Start counting the hours as you pass them, 10:00, 11:00, 12:00. Remind the class that when you get to 12:00, the time begins again at 1:00, since there are two 12-hour sections in one day. Continue counting until you get to 3:00 (six hours of elapsed time).

5. Ask a student to read the question in the second section of the reference sheet. Ask the following question:

   ✳ What strategy can we use to find what time Mom placed the ham in the oven? *(counting back)*

   Count back, starting at 2:00 on the Judy clock and moving the hour hand backward as the students count: 1:00, 12:00, 11:00. Ask the following question:

   ✳ What time did Mom place the ham in the oven? *(11:00)*

6. Place the students in pairs. Distribute the "Find the Time" worksheet and display the transparency. Read the directions with the students. Distribute Judy clocks to each pair for their use in solving the problems. Circulate the room, monitoring their progress. When the pairs have completed the worksheet, ask for volunteers to explain how each problem was solved. Collect the Judy clocks.

7. Direct the class's attention to the times on the board. Remind them that this shows the time the volunteer began and finished an activity. Ask the students how long the student did the activity. *(Answers will vary.)*

8. Distribute the "The Time Is . . ." worksheet. Read the directions with the class. Have them work on this activity on their own. When they have finished, display the transparency and review the answers.

Wrap-Up

To conclude this lesson, have the students write responses using complete sentences to the following prompts in their math journal or on a sheet of notebook paper. Allow adequate time for task completion and then ask various students to share their responses with the class.

   ✳ What is elapsed time? *(the amount of time that passes)*

   ✳ When do you use elapsed time in real life? *(knowing when a movie will be over, knowing what time you will need to go home, etc.)*

Time *(cont.)*

How Much Time?

Question: What time does each of these clocks show?

_____    _____

The first clock shows the time Jeremy went to his friend's house.

The second clock shows the time Jeremy came home.

Question: What is a strategy we can use to find out how long Jeremy played at his friend's house?

Mom baked a ham. When the ham had been in the oven for 3 hours, she took it out. It was 2:00. What time did Mom place the ham in the oven?

Question: What strategy can be used to find out what time Mom placed the ham in the oven?

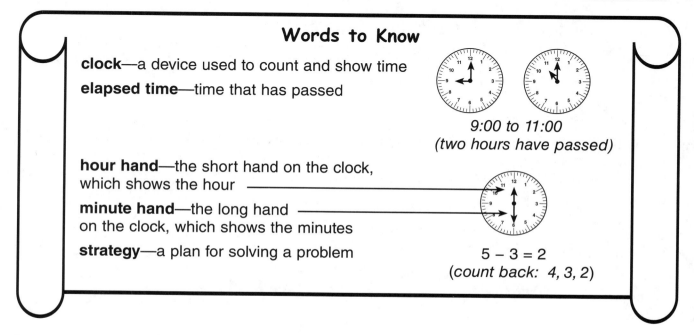

Words to Know

clock—a device used to count and show time

elapsed time—time that has passed

9:00 to 11:00
(two hours have passed)

hour hand—the short hand on the clock, which shows the hour

minute hand—the long hand on the clock, which shows the minutes

strategy—a plan for solving a problem

5 − 3 = 2
(count back: 4, 3, 2)

Time *(cont.)*

Find the Time

Directions: Answer each question by drawing a line to the correct clock or amount of time.

1. The fair opened at 10:00 in the morning and closed at 11:00 that evening. How many hours was the fair open?

| 13 hours |

2. Dylan fed his new puppy at 8:00 in the morning. His mom said he could feed the puppy again in 5 hours. What time will Dylan feed his puppy?

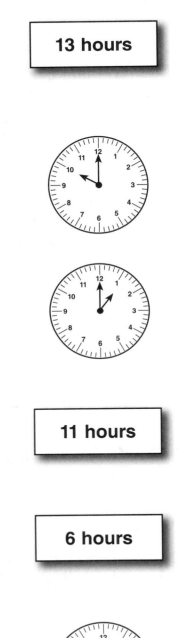

3. Missy played in her tree house for four hours. She climbed down at 2:00. What time did Missy go into her tree house?

4. Jacob fell asleep on the sofa at 4:00. He woke up at 3:00. How long did Jacob sleep?

| 11 hours |

5. Tara was at the zoo from 2:00 until 8:00. How long was Tara at the zoo?

| 6 hours |

6. Pete's family finished decorating the house at 6:00. They had been working on it for 4 hours. What time did they start decorating the house?

Time (cont.)

The Time Is . . .

Directions: Read each problem. Write your answer on the line.

1. Sammy brought his pictures in to have them developed at 7:00. The man said they would be ready in three hours. What time will Sammy's pictures be ready? _____

2. Kelly and Jaime started playing board games at 12:00. They finished at 4:00. How long did they play? _____

3. John was doing research on the computer for 7 hours. He finished at 1:00. What time did John start? _____

4. Michelle went to her grandmother's house at 3:00. She came home at 4:00. How long did Michelle stay at her grandmother's? _____

5. Toni made popsicles. She left them in the freezer for five hours and took them out at 7:00. When did she place them in the freezer? _____

6. Anne spent the afternoon reading in her room. She read from 1:00 until 4:00. How long did Anne read? _____

7. Dad went in the garden to work at 8:00. He worked for three hours. What time did he finish? _____

8. Tim watched a bird build a nest for two hours. The bird flew away at 2:00. What time did the bird start building the nest? _____

Days and Months

Skill 11: The student will list the days of the week and the months in a year in order.

Instructional Preparation

Materials:

- day and month cutout cards (*one set of either day or month cards per team of three or four*)

Duplicate the following (one per student, unless otherwise indicated):

- "Days and Months" reference sheet
- "What's Missing?" worksheet

Prepare an overhead transparency of the following:

- "Days and Months" reference sheet
- "What's Missing?" worksheet

Recall

Before beginning the **Review** component, facilitate a discussion based on these questions:

- ✳ Ask a student when his or her birthday is. (*Answers will vary, for example, March 13.*)
- ✳ What is March? (*a month*)
- ✳ What does the 13 represent? (*the day of the month*)

Review

1. Have the students look at the class calendar. Ask them the following questions:

   - ✳ What month is it? (*for example, October*)
   - ✳ What is today's date? (*for example, the 18th*)
   - ✳ What day of the week is the 18th? (*for example, Wednesday*)

   Explain that today they are going to review the order of the days of the week and the months of the year.

2. Display the "Words to Know" section of the "Days and Months" transparency. Ask for a volunteer to read the first term and definition to the class. Ask the class if they can name all of the days of the week. Write the days on the left side of the board as the class says them. Then have a volunteer read the second term and definition to the class. Ask the class if they can name all of the months of the year. Write these responses on the right side of the board. Now show the class the "Days of the Week" section of the transparency. Have the class read the days of the week aloud with you. Compare the days you wrote on the board with those on the reference sheet. Explain to the class that the reference sheet shows the days of the week in the correct order. Ask this question:

   - ✳ Why is it important to know the correct order of the days of the week?

   Write the days of the week in order on the board. Place your hand over one of the days. Ask the class which day is missing. Do this a few times, using a different day or days.

Days and Months *(cont.)*

Review *(cont.)*

3. Now show the "Months of the Year" section of the transparency. Explain to the students that this shows the months of the year in order, from the first month, January, to the last month, December. Have the class read the months aloud with you. Compare the months the class gave you with those on the reference sheet. Ask this question:

   ✳ Why is it important to know the correct order of the months of the year? (*Answers will vary.*)

   Write the months of the year in order on the board. Place your hand over one of the months. Ask the class which month is missing. Do this a few times using a different month or months. Erase both sides of the board when you are finished.

4. Place the students in groups of three or four. Give each group a set of "Days of the Week" cards or a set of "Months of the Year" cards. Tell each group to mix up the cards and to place them upside-down. When you say "go," have each group turn the cards over and place the cards in a row in the correct order. When each group is finished, distribute the "Days and Months" reference sheet for them to check that they have placed their cards in the correct order. Have the students put away their reference sheets and repeat this activity a few times, making sure all of the members in the group have a chance to place the cards in order. Then have each group that has the "Days of the Week" cards exchange cards with a group that has the "Months of the Year" cards. Repeat this style of practice.

5. Distribute the "What's Missing?" worksheet and display the transparency. Explain to the class that they will be filling in the missing days of the week and months of the year in order. Point out that some of the problems have more than one space to fill in. When the students have finished, have them take out their reference sheets to check their answers and ask for volunteers to write their answers on the transparency.

Wrap-Up

To conclude this lesson, have the students write a response using complete sentences to the following prompts in their math journal or on a sheet of notebook paper. Allow adequate time for task completion and then ask various students to share their responses with the class.

   ✳ How many days are in a week? (*seven*)

   ✳ Write the days of the week in order. (*Sunday, Monday, Tuesday, Wednesday, Thursday, Friday, and Saturday*)

   ✳ How many months are in a year? (*12*)

   ✳ Write the months of the year in order. (*January, February, March, April, May, June, July, August, September, October, November, and December*)

   ✳ Why is it helpful to know the order of the days of the week and months of the year? (*Answers will vary.*)

Days and Months *(cont.)*

Reference Sheet

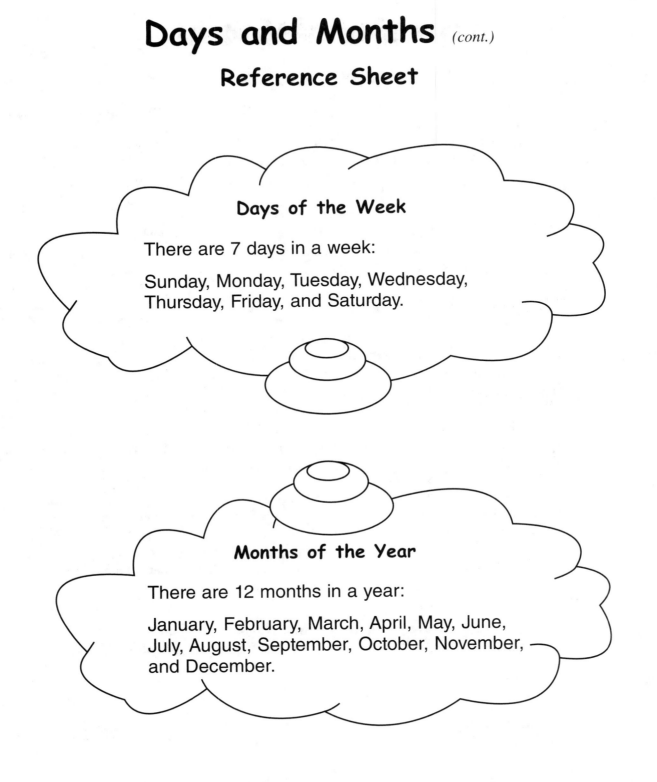

Days of the Week

There are 7 days in a week:

Sunday, Monday, Tuesday, Wednesday, Thursday, Friday, and Saturday.

Months of the Year

There are 12 months in a year:

January, February, March, April, May, June, July, August, September, October, November, and December.

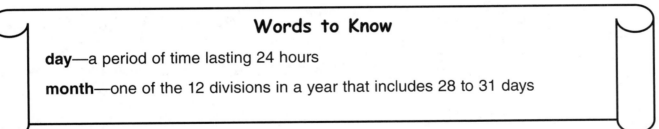

Words to Know

day—a period of time lasting 24 hours

month—one of the 12 divisions in a year that includes 28 to 31 days

Days and Months (cont.)

Cutout Cards

Sunday	April
Monday	May
Tuesday	June
Wednesday	July
Thursday	August
Friday	September
Saturday	October
January	November
February	December
March	

Days and Months *(cont.)*

What's Missing?

Directions: Write the missing day or month on the line.

1. Wednesday, Thursday, Friday, _____ ,

   Sunday, Monday

2. October, November, December, _____ , February

3. April, May, _____ , July, _____ ,

   September

4. _____ , Tuesday, Wednesday, _____

5. February, March, _____ , May

6. _____ , _____ , September,

   October, November

7. Sunday, _____ , Tuesday, Wednesday,

   _____

8. Tuesday, Wednesday, _____ , _____ ,

   Saturday, _____

A.M. and P.M.

Skill 12: The student will use the terms "A.M." and "P.M." appropriately in context.

Instructional Preparation

Materials:

- Judy clock
- scissors (*one pair per student*)

Duplicate the following (one per student, unless otherwise indicated):

- "Before or After?" reference sheet
- "Cutouts" worksheet
- "A.M. or P.M.?" worksheet

Prepare an overhead transparency of the following:

- "Before or After?" reference sheet
- "Situations" reference sheet
- "A.M. or P.M.?" worksheet

Recall

Before beginning the **Review** component, facilitate a discussion based on the following questions:

- ✳ What do we use a calendar for? (*Answers will vary.*)
- ✳ What does a clock tell us? (*the time of day*)

Review

1. Hold up the Judy clock. Ask the students what they see on the clock. (*the hour and minute hands, the numbers 1–12, hash marks, etc.*) Set the clock to show 7:00. Ask a volunteer to tell you the time. Ask the following question:

   - ✳ Is the clock showing 7:00 in the morning or 7:00 in the evening? (*This question can't be answered by only looking at the clock.*)

   Tell them that there is really no way of knowing without more information. Explain to the students that today they will be using the terms "A.M." and "P.M." when telling time.

   Distribute the "Before or After?" reference sheet and display its transparency. Review the terms and definitions in the "Words to Know" section at the bottom of the page. Use the Judy clock to show the class that the hour hand goes completely around the clock two times to complete the 24 hours in a day.

Review (cont.)

2. Direct attention to the top of the reference sheet. Have a volunteer read the question at the top of the page aloud to the class. Explain that this is a similar problem to the one at the beginning of the lesson. An e-mail will show either "A.M." or "P.M." after the time, so you know if it was sent in the morning or the afternoon. With the class, read the definitions of "A.M." and "P.M." Use the Judy clock to count the hours from midnight to 11:59 A.M. and then from noon to 11:59 P.M.

Read the first phrase "In the morning" to the class. Ask the following questions:

* What do you do in the morning? (*waking up, going to school, etc.*)

* How would you write the time you eat breakfast? (*Times will vary but should include "A.M."*)

Write the times given to you on the transparency. Ask for different examples of what the students do in the morning and write the times they are done in the box on the transparency. Ask the following questions each time:

* Is it A.M. or P.M.? (*A.M.*)

* How do you know? (*It is in the morning, and morning is A.M.*)

Follow this format with the rest of the sections. Write the times in the appropriate boxes on the transparency. Remind the class that 12:00 is often not written with "A.M." or "P.M." The words *noon* and *midnight* are used to tell them apart.

4. Distribute scissors and the "Cutouts" worksheet to the students. Have them cut out the two words on the page. Explain that they are going to hear a situation and will need to decide if it happened in the A.M. or P.M. and hold up the correct sign. Display the "Situations" reference sheet and ask different students to read the situations to the class. Create a few more situations if you feel the class needs additional practice.

5. Distribute the "A.M. or P.M.?" worksheet. Tell the class that they will be writing the time on the line and circling either "A.M." or "P.M." Have the students work on this individually. When they have finished, display the transparency and ask for volunteers to share their answers.

Wrap-Up

To conclude this lesson, have the students write responses using complete sentences to the following prompts in their math journal or on a sheet of notebook paper. Allow adequate time for task completion and then ask various students to share their responses with the class.

* What time period is A.M.? (*from midnight until 11:59, just before noon*)

* What time period is P.M.? (*from noon until 11:59, just before midnight*)

* Why is it important to know the difference between A.M. and P.M.? (*Answers will vary.*)

A.M. and P.M. *(cont.)*

Before or After?

Question: My friend sent me an e-mail at 3:30. Did she send me the e-mail at 3:30 in the morning or 3:30 in the afternoon?

A.M. is the time from 12:00 (midnight) until 11:59, just before noon.

Sweet Dreams

Rise and Shine

P.M. is the time from 12:00 (noon) until 11:59, just before midnight

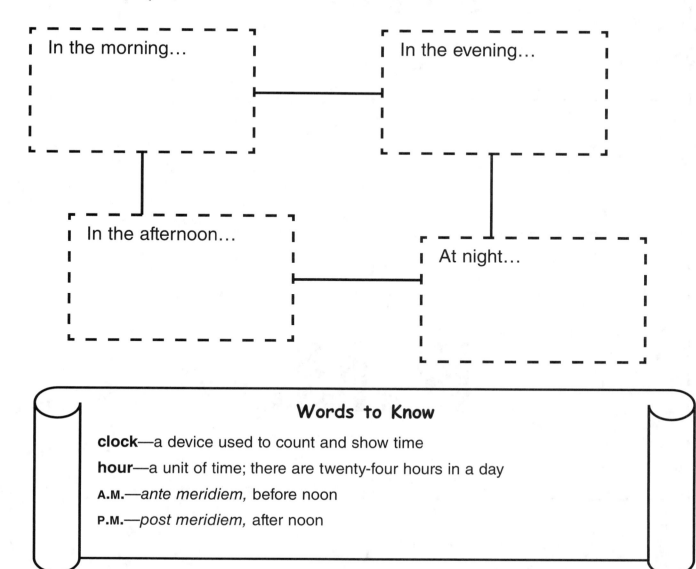

In the morning…

In the evening…

In the afternoon…

At night…

Words to Know

clock—a device used to count and show time

hour—a unit of time; there are twenty-four hours in a day

A.M.—*ante meridiem,* before noon

P.M.—*post meridiem,* after noon

Cutouts

A.M.

P.M.

74

A.M. and P.M. *(cont.)*

Situations

1. When I took my dog for a walk, the sun was just coming up.	**6.** We went swimming in the pool an hour after lunch.
2. It was dark out when I took out the trash. It was really late at night.	**7.** Grandpa gave me a dish of ice cream because I finished my dinner.
3. My dad woke me up early to go fishing.	**8.** We were on the beach as the sun set.
4. My mom made lunch at 1:00.	**9.** We took our spelling test when we first got to school.
5. I practiced my spelling words until bedtime.	**10.** I make my bed before I get dressed in the morning.

A.M. and P.M. *(cont.)*

A.M. or P.M.?

Directions: Read each situation. Then write the time on the line and circle "A.M." or "P.M."

1. Harold went to the park with his aunt. They got home at 5:30, just in time for supper!	_____ A.M. _____ P.M.
2. Sadie went to the store with her mom. They got there right when it opened at 10:30.	_____ A.M. _____ P.M.
3. The movie began at 11:45, right before midnight.	_____ A.M. _____ P.M.
4. Amy finished the last page of her coloring book at 8:30, just when her mom told her to start getting ready for bed.	_____ A.M. _____ P.M.
5. When he was on his brother's boat, Tony saw the sun rise at 5:25.	_____ A.M. _____ P.M.
6. It was 9:10 on Wednesday when the moon went behind the cloud. Everything got dark.	_____ A.M. _____ P.M.
7. What time did you go to bed last night?	_____ A.M. _____ P.M.
8. What time do you have lunch at school?	_____ A.M. _____ P.M.
9. Terri started reading her book at 12:10, just after noon.	_____ A.M. _____ P.M.
10. Bob woke up because the baby was crying. It was 1:05, about an hour past midnight.	_____ A.M. _____ P.M.

Dollars and Cents

Skill 13: The student will write money values using the cent and dollar signs and decimals.

Instructional Preparation

Materials:

- overhead money; bills and coins
- scissors (*one pair per group of 3–4 students*)
- "Money Amounts" sheet

Duplicate the following (one per student, unless otherwise indicated):

- "Dollars and Cents" reference sheet
- "Cutouts" (*one per group of 3–4 students*)
- "Money—It's All $ and ¢" worksheet

Prepare an overhead transparency of the following:

- "Dollars and Cents" reference sheet
- "Money—It's All $ and ¢" worksheet

Recall

Before beginning the **Review** component, facilitate a discussion based on the following qupant to buy an apple at the store, what do you give the cashier? *(money)*

　　✳ What different kinds of money could you give the cashier? *(bills and coins)*

Review

1. Place two one-dollar bills, one dime, one nickel, and two pennies on the overhead. Tell the class this is how much money you found in your drawer. Add the money together as a class and write the total amount on the overhead above the money. (*$2.17*) Explain to the class that today they are going to write money amounts using dollar and cent signs.

2. Distribute the "Dollars and Cents" reference sheet and display the transparency. Review the "Words to Know" section at the bottom of the page by having volunteers read the terms and definitions. Then direct attention to the top of the page.

3. Read the information in the "Dollar Sign(s)" section while the students follow along. Show the money you used in step 1 on the overhead and ask the following question:

　　✳ How would you write the money found in the drawer using these steps? (*$2.17*)

   Show different amounts of money on the overhead and practice using the dollar sign with just bills, bills and coins, and just coins. Give an example using an amount less than 10 cents. Explain to the class that a zero is placed in front of the amount—for example, "$0.04."

Dollars and Cents *(cont.)*

Review *(cont.)*

4. When you feel the class is comfortable using the dollar sign, redisplay the transparency and read the "Cent Sign (¢)" section with the class. Count the coins together and write 48¢ on the line. Ask the following question:

   ✳ How can this amount be written using a dollar sign? *($0.48)*

   Read the "Remember" section aloud as a class. Ask the following questions:

   ✳ When can you use a dollar sign to write an amount of money? *(You can use a dollar sign every time.)*

   ✳ When can you use a cent sign to write an amount of money? *(You can use the cent sign when you have less than a dollar.)*

   ✳ When can you use a decimal? *(only when you use a dollar sign)*

   ✳ How can 43 cents be written two different ways? *($0.43 and 43¢)*

5. Place the students in groups of 3–4 and give each group a "Cutouts" sheet. Ask each group to cut out the numbers and symbols and place them face up. When each team is ready, read one of the amounts from the "Money Amounts" page. Have each team show that amount of money using the dollar and/or cent sign(s). Explain that some of the amounts will need to be shown in two different ways. Allow the students to use their "Dollars and Cents" reference sheet to help them. Add more amounts if you feel it is necessary. Have them return to their desks when this activity is completed.

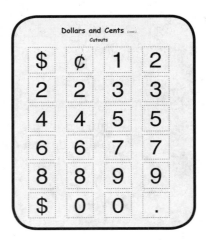

6. Distribute the "Money—It's All $ and ¢" worksheet and display the transparency. Read the directions for the first section with them. Have them work on this section individually. When they have finished, read the second set of directions with them and have them also complete this section individually. When the students have completed this section, ask for volunteers to share their answers and mark them on the transparency.

Wrap-Up

To conclude this lesson, have the students write responses using complete sentences to the following prompts in their math journal or on a sheet of notebook paper. Allow adequate time for task completion and then ask various students to share their responses with the class.

   ✳ Explain and show how to write 31 cents using the dollar sign, cent sign, and decimal. *(A dollar sign is used with a decimal, so 31 cents is written as $0.31. A cent sign is used only with amounts less than a dollar, so it is written as 31¢.)*

   ✳ When would this skill be used in everyday life? *(Answers will vary.)*

Dollars and Cents *(cont.)*

Reference Sheet

Dollar Sign ($)

Dollars are whole numbers.

When you write a dollar amount, follow these steps:

1. Write a dollar sign. $
2. Write the number of dollars. $4
3. Write a decimal. $4.
4. If you have no coins, you could write $4 or you could write $4.00.
5. If you *do* have coins, you write the amount of the coins. $4.13

Cents are less than a whole dollar.

When you have only coins, you can write the amount using a dollar sign by following these steps:

1. Write a dollar sign. $
2. Write the number of dollars. $0
3. Write a decimal. $0.
4. Write the amount of cents you have. $0.56

Cent Sign (¢)

You use the cent sign only when the amount you are writing is less than one dollar.

How much money is shown here?

Write the amount with a cent sign *after* the amount. _____

Remember: You can use only one sign. A dollar sign uses a decimal, and a cent sign does not.

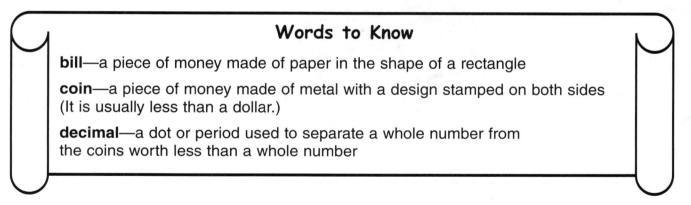

Words to Know

bill—a piece of money made of paper in the shape of a rectangle

coin—a piece of money made of metal with a design stamped on both sides (It is usually less than a dollar.)

decimal—a dot or period used to separate a whole number from the coins worth less than a whole number

Dollars and Cents *(cont.)*

Money Amounts

Directions: Place the students in groups of 3–4. Distribute the "Cutouts" page to each group. Read each of the following amounts. Have each group show the amount using their cutouts. Some amounts will need to be shown in two different ways.

$3.18	85¢
$12.01	40¢
35¢	$1.93
9¢	$10.01
$20.20	$3.85
$11.24	3¢

Dollars and Cents (cont.)
Cutouts

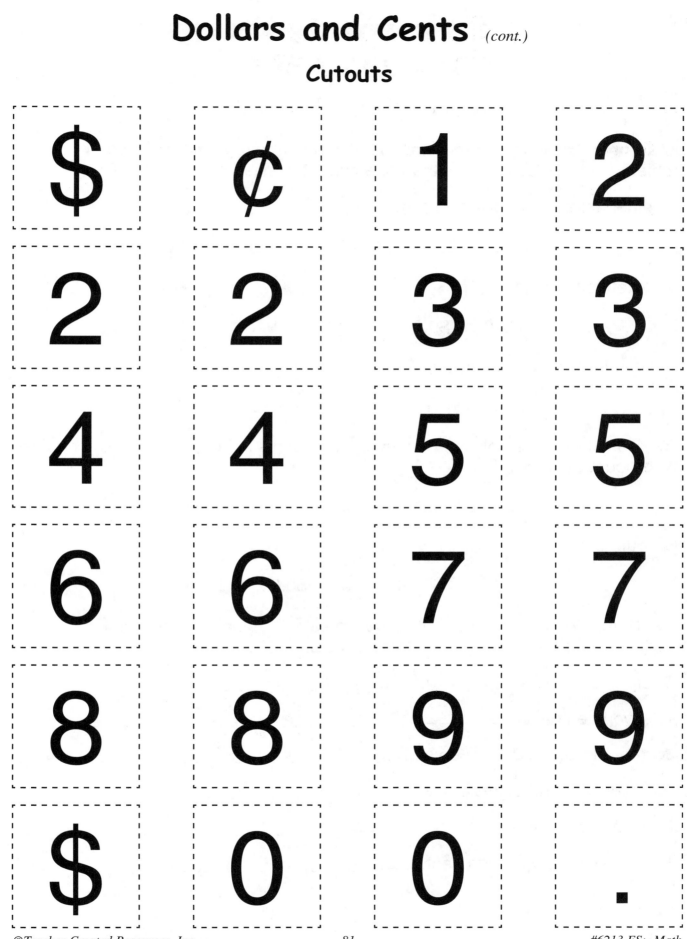

Name: _____

Dollars and Cents *(cont.)*

Money—It's All $ and ¢

Directions: Circle the correct way to write the amount of money in each problem. There may be more than one correct answer.

1. eight dollars and forty-two cents

$8.42 $842 $84.2 $8.42¢   8.42¢

2. ninety-one cents

$9.10 $0.91 $0.91¢   91¢   ¢ 91

3. one dollar and one cent

$1.1 $0.11   1.01¢ $1.01¢ $1.01

4. Tiffany has three dollars and twenty-three cents in her pocket. How can this amount be shown?

$3.23¢   3.23¢ $3.23 $32.3 $323

5. four cents

$4.00 $0.40   4¢ $0.04 $.04¢

Directions: Write the amount of money in each problem on the line. If there are two lines, write the amount two different ways.

6. eighteen dollars ⟶ _____

7. seventeen cents ⟶ _____   _____

8. three dollars and four cents ⟶ _____

9. ten dollars and eighty cents ⟶ _____

10. twenty-four cents ⟶ _____   _____

11. six dollars and sixteen cents ⟶ _____

Adding and Subtracting

Skill 14: The student will add and subtract whole numbers with regrouping.

Instructional Preparation

Materials:

- 50 pennies in a jar
- blank transparency sheet

Duplicate the following (one per student, unless otherwise indicated):

- "Adding and Subtracting" reference sheet
- "Heads or Tails" worksheet (*one per student pair*)
- "Watch the Signs!" worksheet

Prepare an overhead transparency of the following:

- "Adding and Subtracting" reference sheet
- "Heads or Tails" worksheet
- "Watch the Signs!" worksheet

Recall

Before beginning the **Review** component, facilitate a discussion based on these questions:

- ✳ What are some different things we can do with numbers? (*Answers will vary.*)
- ✳ When do we use numbers outside the classroom? (*buying a snack, making a phone call, etc.*)

Review

1. Show the class the jar of pennies. Ask how they can find the number of pennies in the jar. Lead the discussion to grouping the pennies into tens, and then show students how they can simply count by tens to find the total. Explain that today they are going be adding and subtracting with regrouping.

2. Distribute the "Adding and Subtracting" reference sheet and display the transparency. Review the terms and definitions in the "Words to Know" section with the class.

3. Direct attention to the "Let's Add!" section. Ask a volunteer to read the "Remember" section. Now focus attention on problem #1. Ask the following questions:

   - ✳ Since you always begin in the ones column, which numbers should you add first? (*4 and 5*)
   - ✳ What is the sum of 4 and 5? (*9*)

   Model writing the number "9" in the ones column and have the students write it on their paper. Tell the class that they will now add the next column, the tens column. Ask the following question:

   - ✳ What is the sum of 8 and 1? (*9*)

   Model writing the number "9" in the tens column and have the students write it on their paper. Ask the following question:

   - ✳ What is the sum of 84 and 15? (*99*)

Adding and Subtracting *(cont.)*

Review *(cont.)*

Now do problem #2 as a class. Ask the following questions:

✳ What numbers do we add first? *(7 and 5)*

✳ What is the sum of 7 and 5? *(12)*

Explain that when the answer is more than 9, we need to write down the number of ones in the ones column. Model writing "2" and have the students do the same. Explain that the "1" means there is 1 ten, so they carry that number to the tens column. Write a "1" above the "5" and have the students do the same. Now tell them that they will be adding all the tens together: 1 + 5 + 2. Write "8" in the tens column. Ask:

✳ What is the sum of 57 and 25? *(82)*

Ask the students to solve problem #3 on their own. Then ask the following:

✳ Which numbers did you add first? *(8 and 7)* Why? *(They are in the ones column.)*

✳ What is the sum of 8 and 7? *(15)*

✳ How do you write this number? *(You write the 5 in the ones column and carry the 1 ten to the tens column.)*

✳ What is the next step? *(adding 1, 6, and 3 in the tens column)*

✳ What is this sum? *(10)*

Write the "0" in the tens column. Then explain to the students that since there is no other column to add, the 1 hundred is written in the answer.

✳ What is this sum of 68 and 37? *(105)*

Write the problem "458 + 305" on a blank transparency. Have them copy this problem on the back of their page and solve it on their own. When they are finished, ask them questions in a style similar to that of the earlier questions. Remind the class that the procedure does not change if there are more or less numbers to add or subtract.

4. Now have the class look at the "Let's Subtract!" section. Have a volunteer read the "Remember" section. Focus the students' attention on problem #4. Tell them that when they subtract, they will also start in the ones column. Ask the following question:

✳ What is 4 from 5? *(1)*

Model writing the difference in the ones column. Ask the following questions:

✳ What do we do next? *(subtract the numbers in the tens column)*

✳ What is the difference between 4 and 1? *(3)*

Write the "3" in the tens column and have the students do the same. Ask:

✳ What is the difference between 45 and 14? *(31)*

Now do problem #5 with the class. Ask the following question:

✳ What is 2 minus 5? *(You can't take 5 from 2.)*

Explain that 1 ten will need to be regrouped into 10 ones and placed in the ones column. Cross out the "5" and write a "4." Then write a small "1" before the "2" and explain that now there are 12 ones.

Remind the class that the value of the number did not change; the amounts were just grouped in a different way. Now ask the class the difference between 12 and 5. *(7)* Write "7" in the ones column and have the students do the same. Tell the class that now they need to move to the tens column and subtract 2 from 4. Ask the class for the difference and write this in the tens column (2). Ask the following question:

✳ What is the difference between 52 and 25? *(27)*

Adding and Subtracting *(cont.)*

Review *(cont.)*

Have the students look at problem #6. Ask the following questions:

❋ What is 6 from 4? (*You can't take 6 from 4.*)

❋ What do you need to do? (*borrow*)

Explain that when there is nothing to borrow, they need to go to the next column, the hundreds column, and borrow 1 hundred. Cross out the "2" and make it a "1." Then add the 1 hundred to the tens column, so it now has 10 tens. Explain that they can now borrow 1 ten from the tens column. Cross out the "10" and write "9." Then place a "1" next to the "4," showing 14 ones.

Write the problem "804 – 165" on the blank transparency. Have the students copy this on the back of their page. Have them solve this problem on their own. When they are finished, go over the steps involved, including going to the hundreds column to borrow. If you feel it is necessary, do a few additional problems with them.

5. Place the students in pairs. Give each pair a penny and the "Heads or Tails" worksheet. Read the directions with the students. Circulate the room and monitor them as they solve the problems. Remind them to write the sign used on each problem. When the pairs are finished, collect the pennies and display the transparency. Have the students help you solve each problem, first showing addition and then showing subtraction. Ask the class what they did when they needed to borrow two times for one problem. Did they solve it correctly? Answer any questions the students have. Then have them return to their seats.

6. Distribute the "Watch the Signs!" worksheet. Read the directions with the class. Explain that showing their work means showing when they regroup or carry digits from one column to another. Remind them to pay attention to the signs; some of the problems are addition and some are subtraction. Have them work on this independently. When finished, display the transparency and review the way each of the problems is solved.

Wrap-Up

To conclude this lesson, have the students write responses using complete sentences to the following prompts in their math journal or on a sheet of notebook paper. Allow adequate time for task completion and then ask various students to share their responses with the class.

❋ Explain what to do when you are adding and the sum of two of the digits is more than 9. Show an example. (*Answers may include the ones and tens columns—writing down the digit in the ones column and bringing the "ten" over to the next column. This number then gets added to the column.*)

$$\begin{array}{r} 36 \\ + 17 \\ \hline 53 \end{array}$$

❋ Explain what to do when you are subtracting and you need to borrow from the next column. Show an example. (*Answers should include regrouping the next larger column, for example, the tens, and bringing 1 ten to the ones column.*)

$$\begin{array}{r} 36 \\ - 17 \\ \hline 19 \end{array}$$

❋ Why do you need to know these skills? (*Answers will vary. Examples include using addition and subtraction in our daily lives when balancing a checkbook, building, or making a purchase.*)

Adding and Subtracting *(cont.)*

Reference Sheet

Let's Add!

Remember: When you add numbers, you always start in the ones column.

1.

tens	ones
8	4
+ 1	5

2.

tens	ones
5	7
+ 2	5

3.

hundreds	tens	ones
	6	8
+	3	7

Let's Subtract!

Remember: When you subtract, always place the larger number on top.

4.

tens	ones
4	5
− 1	4

5.

tens	ones
5	2
− 2	5

6.

hundreds	tens	ones
2	0	4
−	1	6

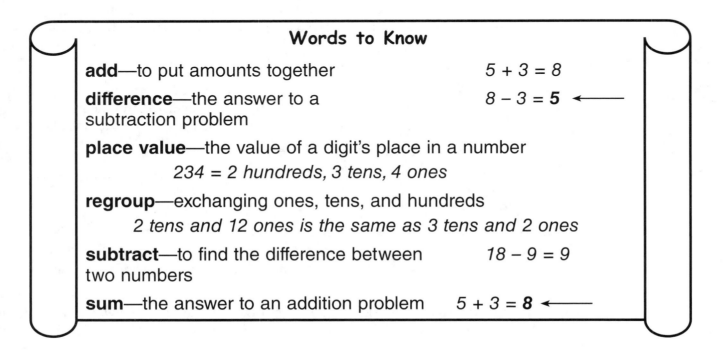

Words to Know

add—to put amounts together $\qquad 5 + 3 = 8$

difference—the answer to a
subtraction problem $\qquad 8 - 3 = 5 \longleftarrow$

place value—the value of a digit's place in a number
$\qquad 234 = 2$ *hundreds, 3 tens, 4 ones*

regroup—exchanging ones, tens, and hundreds
$\qquad$ *2 tens and 12 ones is the same as 3 tens and 2 ones*

subtract—to find the difference between $\qquad 18 - 9 = 9$
two numbers

sum—the answer to an addition problem $\qquad 5 + 3 = 8 \longleftarrow$

Name: _____

Adding and Subtracting *(cont.)*

Heads or Tails

Directions: The person going first flips the penny.

✳ **Heads** = the problem is solved using addition.

✳ **Tails** = the problem is solved using subtraction.

Continue taking turns flipping the coin and solving each of the problems in order. Write the sign on each problem. Good luck!

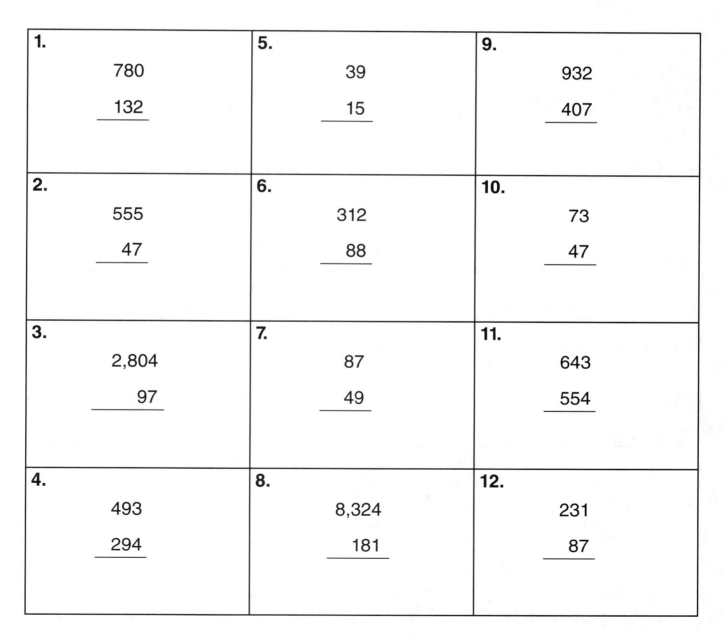

1.
 	
    780
 	
    132
   _____
	5.
	
	    39
	
	    15
	   _____
		9.
		
		    932
		
		    407
		   _____

2.
 	
    555
 	
    47
   _____
	6.
	
	    312
	
	    88
	   _____
		10.
		
		    73
		
		    47
		   _____

3.
 	
    2,804
 	
    97
   _____
	7.
	
	    87
	
	    49
	   _____
		11.
		
		    643
		
		    554
		   _____

4.
 	
    493
 	
    294
   _____
	8.
	
	    8,324
	
	    181
	   _____
		12.
		
		    231
		
		    87
		   _____

Name: _____

Adding and Subtracting *(cont.)*

Watch the Signs!

Directions: Solve each problem. Show your work.

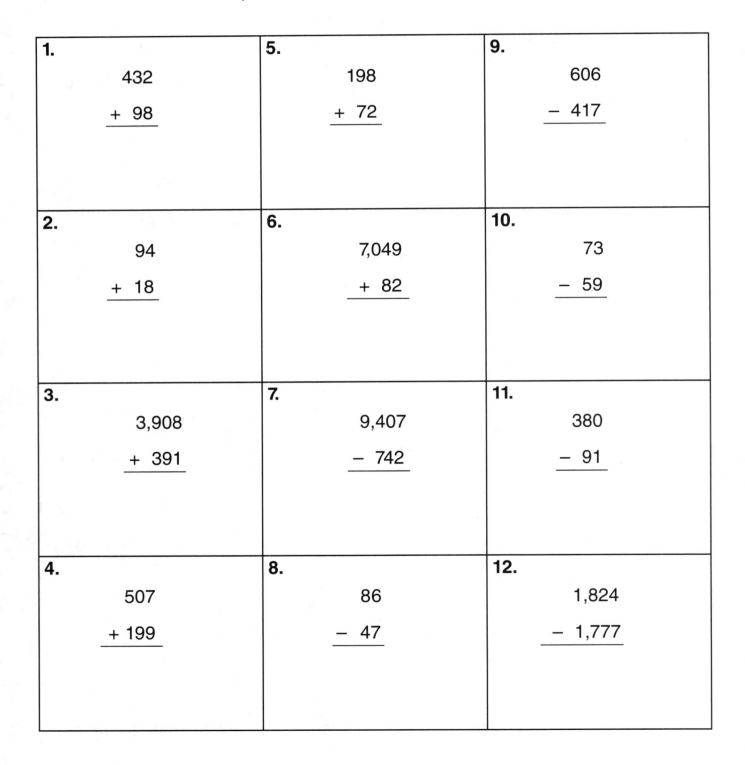

1. 432 + 98	5. 198 + 72	9. 606 − 417
2. 94 + 18	6. 7,049 + 82	10. 73 − 59
3. 3,908 + 391	7. 9,407 − 742	11. 380 − 91
4. 507 + 199	8. 86 − 47	12. 1,824 − 1,777

Fact Families

Skill 15: The student will apply the concept of inverses in fact families.

Instructional Preparation

Duplicate the following (one per student, unless otherwise indicated):

- "It's All in the Family" reference sheet
- "A Family of Facts" worksheet
- "Fact Families and Inverses" worksheet

Prepare an overhead transparency of the following:

- "It's All in the Family" reference sheet
- "A Family of Facts" worksheet
- "Fact Families and Inverses" worksheet

Recall

Before beginning the **Review** component, facilitate a discussion based on the following question:

✳ How can you check to see if your answer to an equation is correct? (*Answers may include redoing the problem, asking a parent, using a calculator, and checking the inverse or opposite operation.*)

Review

1. Ask the following question:

   ✳ What does the word *opposite* mean? (*Accept all reasonable responses.*)

   Say the following words and have the class respond with a word that means the opposite: tall (*short*), big (*little*), hot (*cold*), funny (*sad*), etc. Explain that there are also opposites in math. Write the equation "4 + 6 = 10" on the board. Ask the following questions:

   ✳ What kind of number sentence is this? (*an addition number sentence*)

   ✳ What is the opposite of addition? (*subtraction*)

   Explain that the opposite operation can be used to check if a problem is correct. Tell the students that today they are going to use the opposite operations to check problems and review fact families.

2. Distribute the "It's All in the Family" reference sheet and display the transparency. Direct attention to the "Words to Know" section at the bottom of the page. Review the terms and definitions.

Fact Families *(cont.)*

Review *(cont.)*

3. Now direct attention to the top of the page. Read through the top box as a class. Emphasize that a fact family always uses the same three numbers and two opposite operations (*addition and subtraction or multiplication and division*).

   Read the oval section of the reference sheet. Point to one of the equations in the outer ovals and ask the following questions:

   ✳ Does this number sentence belong to the same fact family as $409 + 17 = 426$? Why or why not? (*Equations that are members of the same fact family: $426 - 409 = 17$, $17 + 409 = 426$, $426 - 17 = 409$.*)

   Continue this style of questioning for each of the remaining equations.

4. Read the remaining section of the reference page. Tell the class that for some students it is easier to solve an addition problem than a subtraction problem; for others, it is the opposite. Therefore, checking a problem by using the inverse can be helpful.

5. Place the students in pairs. Distribute the "A Family of Facts" worksheet and display the transparency. Read the directions for the first section with the pairs. Have them complete this section as you monitor them. When each pair has finished, read the directions for the second section with the class. Circulate around the room as the students work on this section. When they have completed this section, read the directions for the last section. When the pairs have finished, ask for volunteers to share their answers and show their work on the transparency. Have the students return to their seats.

6. Distribute the "Fact Families and Inverses" worksheet. Have the students work on this paper individually. When they have finished, display the transparency and ask volunteers to share their answers by writing them on the transparency.

Wrap-Up

To conclude this lesson, have the students write a response using complete sentences to the following prompts in their math journal or on a sheet of notebook paper. Allow adequate time for task completion and then ask various students to share their responses with the class.

   ✳ What is a fact family? (*a set of related addition and subtraction problems*)

   ✳ When can using an inverse be helpful? (*to check your work*)

   ✳ How can understanding fact families and inverses help you in daily life? (*Answers will vary but may include when making a purchase and when measuring.*)

Fact Families *(cont.)*

It's All in the Family!

Look at this addition sentence: ⟶ 8 + 13 = 21.

Another way to write this sentence is like this: ⟶ 13 + 8 = 21

They are both in the *same* fact family.

The opposite, or inverse, of each of these number sentences are also part of this fact family.

$\begin{cases} 21 - 13 = 8 \\ 21 - 8 = 13 \end{cases}$

Remember: A fact family always uses the same numbers!

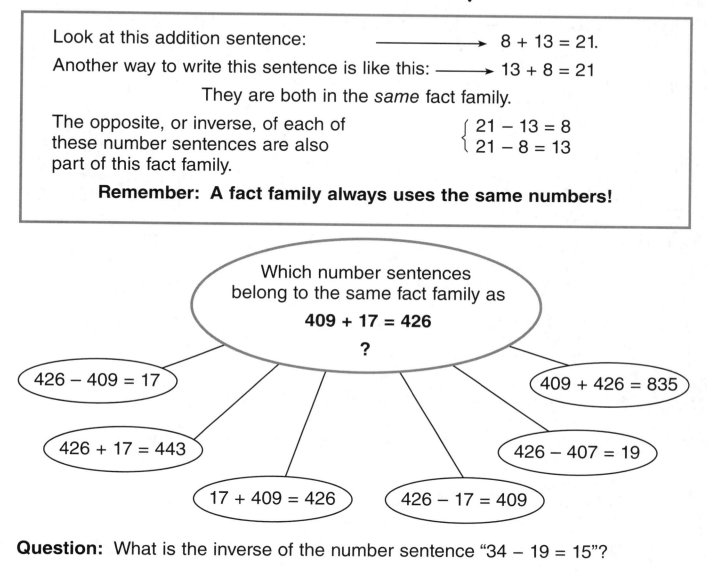

Which number sentences belong to the same fact family as

409 + 17 = 426

?

426 − 409 = 17

409 + 426 = 835

426 + 17 = 443

426 − 407 = 19

17 + 409 = 426

426 − 17 = 409

Question: What is the inverse of the number sentence "34 − 19 = 15"?

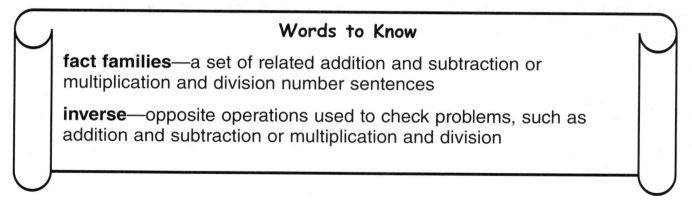

Words to Know

fact families—a set of related addition and subtraction or multiplication and division number sentences

inverse—opposite operations used to check problems, such as addition and subtraction or multiplication and division

Names: _____

Fact Families *(cont.)*

A Family of Facts

Directions: Circle the fact that is missing from each fact family and write the number sentence on the line.

1. 93 + 21 = 114   114 − 93 = 21

   21 + 93 = 114   _____

2. 221 − 105 = 116   116 + 105 = 221

   105 + 116 = 221   _____

3. 15 + 45 = 60   60 − 45 = 15

   45 + 15 = 60   _____

| 114 − 21 = 93 |
| 114 + 21 = 135 |
| 93 − 21 = 72 |

| 116 − 105 = 11 |
| 221 − 116 = 105 |
| 221 − 105 = 326 |

| 60 + 45 = 105 |
| 45 + 60 = 105 |
| 60 − 15 = 45 |

Directions: Look at each set of number sentences. Circle the equations that form a fact family.

4.
   19 + 10 = 29   29 + 10 = 39   29 − 10 = 19   29 − 19 = 10

   29 + 29 = 58   10 + 19 = 29   29 + 19 = 48   19 − 10 = 9

5.
   3 + 7 = 10   17 − 10 = 7   10 + 10 = 20   10 − 3 = 7

   7 − 3 = 4   10 − 7 = 3   7 + 3 = 10   3 + 10 = 13

Directions: Write on the line(s) the missing number sentence or sentences that will complete each fact family.

6. 831 + 128 = 959   128 + 831 = 959   959 − 128 = 831   _____

7. 37 + 49 = 86   86 − 37 = 49   _____   _____

8. 90 − 31 = 59   _____   _____   _____

Fact Families (cont.)

Fact Families and Inverses

Directions: Write your answer to each question on the line provided.

1. Write a number sentence that can be used to check this problem:
$15 + 68 = 83$.

_____

2. Write the number sentences that are part of this fact family: $44 - 13 = 31$.

_____   _____

_____

3. Write the equation that is missing from this family of facts:

$3,756 + 1,100 = 4,856$ $4,856 - 1,100 = 3,756$

$4,856 - 3,756 = 1,100$ _____

4. What is the inverse of "$505 - 500 = 5$"?

_____

5. Sam wrote the following number sentences on his paper. He said they
belong to the same fact family. Is Sam correct? Why or why not?

$49 + 12 = 61$ $49 - 12 = 37$ $61 - 12 = 49$ $12 + 49 = 61$

_____

_____

6. Write your own fact family on the lines below.

_____   _____

_____   _____

Adding and Subtracting by Tens

Skill 16: The student will apply the concept of 10 more or 10 less than a given number.

Instructional Preparation

Duplicate the following (one per student, unless otherwise indicated):

- "More or Less" reference sheet
- "Add 10, Subtract 10" worksheet (*one per student pair*)
- "10 is the Number" worksheet

Prepare an overhead transparency of the following:

- "More or Less" reference sheet
- "Add 10, Subtract 10" worksheet
- "10 is the Number" worksheet

Recall

Before beginning the **Review** component, facilitate a discussion based on these questions:

    ✶ Why do we use numbers? (*Answers will vary.*)

    ✶ What can the digits in numbers tell us? (*Answers may vary.*)

Review

1. Have all the students in the class stand up. Ask a student how many of his or her classmates are standing. Then ask a group of 10 students to sit down without saying the word "ten." Ask a different student to tell you how many students are now standing. Ask a volunteer to tell you the difference between the two numbers. Have 10 more students take a seat without saying the word "ten" and ask the same two questions again. Have the rest of the students sit down and facilitate a discussion comparing all the numbers that were just given and how they all can be explained as 10 more than or 10 less than each other.

2. Distribute the "More or Less" reference sheet and display the transparency. Read the term *place value* in the "Words to Know" section with the class and review the definition.

3. Read the information in the top section. Review the place value of each digit in the number "814." Remind the class that if there were no tens or ones, a zero would be used as a placeholder.

   Direct attention to the first question on the reference sheet:

       ✶ What does the number "814" become when 10 more are added? (*824*)

       ✶ Which place value digit is changed? (*The 1 in the tens column is changed to a 2.*)

   Write these answers on the transparency while the students write them on their paper. Explain to the class that since 1 ten is added, the number in the tens column goes up by one digit.

4. Ask a volunteer to read the next question, "What is the new number when 10 are taken away from the number 814?" Remind them that they need to pay attention to the tens column to answer this question. Ask for a volunteer to answer this question and write this answer on the line as the students write the answer on their paper. (*804*)

Adding and Subtracting by Tens *(cont.)*

Review *(cont.)*

5. Point out this new number, 804. Tell the students that you want to take 10 away from this number; however, there are no tens in the tens column. Remind the students that you need to regroup the hundreds column in order to do this. Since there are 8 hundreds, you will borrow one of them, leaving 7 in the hundreds column. Move that 100 to the tens column. Now you can take away 1 ten, leaving you a new number of 794. Show this process in the box on the transparency.

   Explain to the class that this same process is used when adding 10. If more than 9 units are in the tens place, they will need to be regrouped into the hundreds column. Write the number 192. Tell the class that you want to add 10 to this number; so regrouping is needed. Explain that when 1 ten is added to the 9, that leaves 10 in the tens column. Place a zero in the tens place and add the 1 ten to the hundreds column, giving you a new number of 202. Show this process in the box on the transparency.

6. Direct attention to the final section on the reference sheet. Ask the following questions about the number 96:

   ✳ Which digit is in the ones place? *(6)*

   ✳ Which digit is in the tens place? *(9)*

   ✳ Which column changes when you add 10 to this number? *(the tens column)*

   Ask a volunteer to explain how the number 96 changes to 106. *(The response should include adding 1 ten to the 9, giving you 10 tens. Change the 9 to a 0 and add 1 ten to the hundreds column, for an answer of 106.)*

7. Distribute the "Add 10, Subtract 10" worksheet and display the transparency. Read the directions to the class and model the first problem. What is "57 plus 10"? Write "67" on the line as the students write it on their paper. Explain that they will be adding 10 to each number to make the next number *(77, 87)*. Tell the class that for this section, questions 2–5, they will be adding 10. For questions 6–10, they will be subtracting 10 each time. Place the students into pairs for this activity. Monitor each pair to ensure understanding. When finished, ask for volunteers to share their answers and write them on the transparency.

8. Distribute the "10 is the Number" worksheet. Read the directions with the class. Have the students work on this individually. When they have finished, display the transparency and review the answers.

Wrap-Up

To conclude this lesson, have the students write responses using complete sentences to the following prompts in their math journal or on a sheet of notebook paper. Allow adequate time for task completion and then ask various students to share their responses with the class.

   ✳ Why is it important to know how to add and subtract 10 from different numbers? *(Answers will vary.)*

   ✳ When will you use this skill in everyday life? *(Answers will vary.)*

Adding and Subtracting by Tens *(cont.)*

More or Less

Each digit in the number 814 represents a place value.

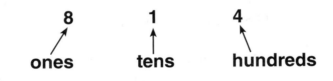

What does the number 814 become when 10 more are added?

Which place value digit is changed?

What is the new number when 10 are taken away from the number 814?

Look at the number 96.

Which digit is in the ones place? _____

Which digit is in the tens place? _____

What is the new number when you add 10 to this number? _____

Words to Know

place value—the value of a digit's place in a number

234 = 2 hundreds, 3 tens, and 4 ones

Adding and Subtracting by Tens *(cont.)*

Add 10, Subtract 10

Directions:

- Add 10 to the number.

- Write this new number on the line.

- Keep adding 10 more on each line.

1. 57   _____   _____   _____

2. 340   _____   _____   _____

3. 181   _____   _____   _____

4. 17   _____   _____   _____

5. 509   _____   _____   _____

Directions:

- Subtract 10 from the number.

- Write this new number on the line.

- Keep subtracting 10 each time.

6. 43   _____   _____   _____

7. 692   _____   _____   _____

8. 288   _____   _____   _____

9. 410   _____   _____   _____

10. 376   _____   _____   _____

Name: _____

Adding and Subtracting by Tens *(cont.)*

10 is the Number

Directions: Write your answers on the lines provided.

---

1. Write the number that is 10 less than 81. _____

---

2. What number is 10 less than 107? _____

---

3. Kyle has 10 more rocks than Jeremy. Jeremy has 145 rocks. How many rocks does Kyle have?

_____

---

4. Write the number that is 10 more than 111. _____

---

5. Which number is 10 more than 398? _____

---

6. Alice has 72 feathers. She found 10 more on her vacation. How many feathers does Alice have now?

_____

---

7. Write the number that is 10 less than 12. _____

---

8. The librarian received 806 new books. The third grade checked out 10 of them the first day. How many new books does the librarian have now?

_____

---

9. Write the number that is 10 more than 449. _____

---

10. Riley watched TV for 45 minutes last night. Chase watched 10 minutes less than Riley. For how many minutes did Chase watch TV?

_____

Fractional Parts

Skill 17: The student will identify fractional parts of whole objects.

Instructional Preparation

Materials:

- red, blue, and green chalk

Duplicate the following (*one per student, unless otherwise indicated*):

- "Fractions: Parts of a Whole" reference sheet
- "What Fraction Is Shaded?" worksheet (*one per group*)
- "Name the Fraction" worksheet

Prepare an overhead transparency of *the* following:

- "Fractions: Parts of a Whole" reference sheet
- "What Fraction Is Shaded?" worksheet
- "Name the Fraction" worksheet

Recall

Before beginning the **Review** component, facilitate a discussion based on these questions:

✶ What in this classroom is a whole? (*a chair, a desk, a new pencil, unopened juice, etc.*)

✶ What in this classroom is less than a whole? (*a used crayon, a partially eaten snack, half a piece of paper, etc.*)

Review

1. Begin the lesson by telling the class the story below. As you tell the story, draw the picture on the board.

   Johnny's family went out for dinner last night. They ordered a large pizza. (*Draw a large circle.*) The pizza was cut into eight slices. (*Divide the circle into eight equal pieces.*) Johnny's mom ate one slice (*use blue chalk to shade in one slice*), his dad ate three slices (*use red chalk to shade in three slices*), and Johnny ate two slices (*use green chalk to shade in two slices*).

   Ask the following questions:

   ✶ How many slices of pizza did Johnny's family eat? (*six slices*)

   ✶ How many slices of pizza are left? (*two slices*)

   Tell the class that the amount of pizza eaten and the amount of pizza left over can be described using fractions. Explain that today they are going to use fractions to describe parts of a whole.

2. Distribute the "Fractions: Parts of a Whole" reference sheet and display the transparency. Review the terms and definitions in the "Words to Know" box at the bottom of the page.

Fractional Parts *(cont.)*

Review *(cont.)*

3. Then direct attention to the box at the top of the page. Ask how many slices there were in the pizza that Johnny's family ordered (8) and write the number on the line. Explain that the eight slices equal one whole pizza. Tell the class you are going to be finding the fractional parts of the pizza that Johnny and his family ate. Ask for a volunteer to read the rules in the "Fraction Rule" box. Refer to the pizza drawn on the board as you answer each question as a class. Keep referring to the "Fraction Rule" box as different volunteers answer each question. Write the number of slices and the fractions on the transparency as the students write them on their paper. (*Question 1: one slice, 1/8; Question 2: three slices, 3/8; Question 3: 2/8; Question 4: 6/8; Question 5: 2/8*)

4. Place the students in groups of two or three. Distribute a copy of the "What Fraction Is Shaded?" worksheet to each group. Explain that the question for each problem is the same: "What fraction of the shape is shaded?" Remind each group to use the fraction rule on the reference sheet to help them. Circulate around the room to monitor each group's work. Now have the groups look at the bottom section of the worksheet. This is a matching section. Groups need to match the shaded shape to the correct fraction. Move from group to group to ensure understanding. When they have finished, display the transparency and review the answers. Point out the last shape on the worksheet. Tell the class that if all sections of the figure are shaded, the whole figure is shaded. Explain that when the numerator is the same as the denominator, it equals one. Ask the following questions:

    ✳ What would the fraction be if the entire pizza had been eaten? (*8/8*)

    ✳ What is another way to say 8/8? (*one whole*)

5. Distribute the "Name the Fraction" worksheet. Have the students work on this individually. When the class has finished, display the transparency and ask for volunteers to share their answers.

Wrap-Up

To conclude this lesson, have the students write a response using complete sentences to the following prompts in their math journal or on a sheet of notebook paper. Allow adequate time for task completion and then ask various students to share their responses with the class.

   ✳ What is a fraction? (*a part of a whole*)

   ✳ What does the numerator tell about the fraction? (*It is part of the whole set. It answers the question asked.*)

   ✳ What does the denominator tell about the fraction? (*It tells the total number of equal parts.*)

   ✳ Where do you use fractions in everyday life? (*Answers will vary but may include when getting gasoline or counting the amount of change you receive from a dollar.*)

Fractional Parts *(cont.)*

Fractions: Parts of a Whole

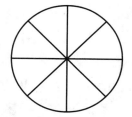

Let's look at the pizza that Johnny's family ate.

How many slices were there in all? _____ slices

So, _____ slices = 1 whole

Fraction Rule

The number that answers the question is the numerator, and it *always* goes above the line.

The total number of equal parts is the denominator, and it *always* goes under the line.

$\dfrac{2}{3}$

Question 1: How many slices did Johnny's mom eat?

- She ate _____ slice
- Let's write this as a fraction.
- How many slices were there altogether? _____ slices
- What fraction of the pizza did Johnny's mom eat? _____

Question 2: What fraction of the pizza did Johnny's dad eat? _____

- How many slices did Johnny's dad eat? _____
- How many slices were there altogether? _____ slices
- What fraction of the pizza did Johnny's dad eat? _____

Question 3: What fraction of the pizza did Johnny eat? _____

Question 4: What fraction of the pizza was eaten? _____

Question 5: What fraction of the pizza was left over? _____

Words to Know

fraction—a number that names part of a whole

whole—an entire amount

numerator—the number above the line in a fraction. It is part of the whole.

denominator—the number below the line in a fraction. It tells the total number of equal parts in the whole.

Fractional Parts *(cont.)*

What Fraction Is Shaded?

Directions: Write on the line the fraction of each shape that is shaded.

1. 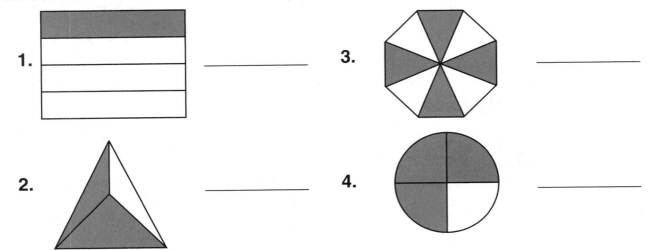 _____

3. _____

2. _____

4. _____

Directions: Draw a line from the fraction to the shaded shape it names.

$\frac{2}{2}$

$\frac{2}{4}$

$\frac{1}{3}$

$\frac{4}{16}$

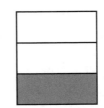

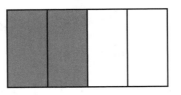

Name: _____

Fractional Parts *(cont.)*

Name the Fraction

Directions: Write the fraction that names the shaded part of the shape on the line. If there is more than one line, there is more than one answer.

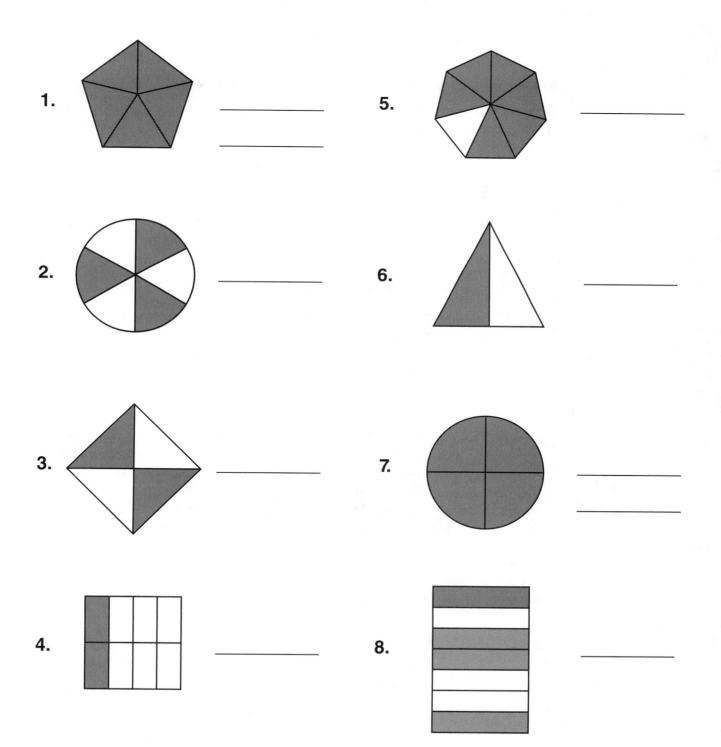

1. _____
   _____

2. _____

3. _____

4. _____

5. _____

6. _____

7. _____
   _____

8. _____

103

Multiplication and Division

Skill 18: The student will identify situations that include multiplication and division, such as equal groups of objects and sharing equally.

Instructional Preparation

Materials:

- stickers (*two per student*)
- scissors
- 1 blue and 1 red crayon for each group

Duplicate the following (one per student, unless otherwise indicated):

- "Is It Equal?" reference sheet
- "Cutouts" page (*each group to receive one set of circles*)
- "= Equal =" worksheet

Prepare an overhead transparency of the following:

- "Is It Equal?" reference sheet
- "= Equal =" worksheet

Recall

Before beginning the **Review** component, facilitate a discussion based on these questions:

- ✳ What does it mean if two students have an equal number of pencils in their desks? (*They each have the same number of pencils.*)
- ✳ If your mom sent treats for you to share equally with your friends, what would you do? (*I would give each friend the same number of treats.*)

Review

1. Tell the students that you have stickers for them that will be equally shared. Begin handing them out to the students, saying, "1 for you, 2 for you, 1 for you, 3 for you." Then stop and ask the students if you are equally sharing the stickers. Collect the stickers you have passed out and explain to the students that today they will be making equal groups and equally sharing. Tell them that after the lesson, you will share the stickers equally among them.

2. Distribute the "Is It Equal?" reference sheet and display the transparency. Review the terms and definitions in the "Words to Know" section with the class.

Review *(cont.)*

3. Direct the students' attention to the top of the reference sheet. Explain to the class how the total number of flowers can be found by using repeated addition (3 + 3 + 3 + 3) or by multiplying the number of flowers by the number of bunches (3 × 4). In the section "Are these groups equal?" draw three tables. Draw two books on each table. Ask the following questions:

   ✳ Are these groups equal? *(yes)*

   ✳ Why or why not? *(because each table has the same number of books)*

   ✳ How can you find the total number of books? *(You can add all the books one at a time, you can add 2 + 2 + 2, or you can multiply the number of tables by the number of books, 3 × 2.)*

   Replace the books with apples. Draw one apple on the first table, two apples on the second table, and three apples on the third table. Then ask the following questions:

   ✳ Are these groups equal? *(no)*

   ✳ Why or why not? *(because each table does not have the same number of apples)*

   ✳ Can the total number of apples be found by adding the same number three times? *(no)*

   ✳ Can the total number of apples be found by multiplying three by the number of apples? *(no)*

   When the students understand the difference between equal and unequal groups, direct their attention to the "Equal Sharing" section of the page.

4. Ask for a volunteer to read the problem aloud. Draw three stick-figure "friends" on the transparency. Make an "X" next to each friend to represent a worm. Continue to place one worm next to each friend until all 18 worms have been shared. Tell the class that the worms have been shared equally. Explain to the students that to find the number of worms each friend would get, they could use repeated subtraction or they could divide. Each way will give them the same answer *(6)*. Ask the following questions:

   ✳ Were the worms equally shared? *(yes)*

   ✳ How do you know? *(because each boy has the same number of worms)*

   Show the class the question about the two boys at the bottom of the page. Tell the class that now the 18 worms need to be equally shared by these two boys. Have them share the worms equally using an "X" to represent each worm. When they have finished, ask for a volunteer to come to the overhead and show how he or she divided the worms. Have the volunteer return to his or her desk and then ask the following question:

   ✳ If you didn't have a picture, how could you find out how many worms each boy would get? *(You could keep subtracting the difference by 2, or you could divide 18 by 2.)*

   Have the class put these papers away.

Multiplication and Division *(cont.)*

Review *(cont.)*

5. Divide the class into groups of 2, 3, and 4. Give each group one set of circles from the "Cutouts" page. Have the groups cut out the circles. Explain that each group needs to share the circles equally among the members of the group. Ask each group to stand after equally sharing the circles. Have these groups share with the class what they did and how many circles each person in the group has. Have these groups sit and ask the groups that could not share equally to stand. Have these groups explain why their circles weren't equally shared. *(because we had one circle left over and 3 people in our group, etc.)*

   Ask each group that wasn't able to share equally to place its circles in a pile and to have one member of the group sit down. Have the group try to share its circles equally without one member. (If this happened with a group containing two students, have a student from a group that was able to equally share its circles join that group.)

   Continue this activity by having groups exchange circles, and when needed, having a student sit down or adding a student, until you feel this concept is understood. Then have these final groups sit together.

6. Distribute a red and blue crayon to each group. Tell the groups to make two red triangles on each circle. Then ask one group to stand up and hold up their circles for the rest of the class to see. Ask the following questions:

   ✳ How many red triangles did you place on each circle? *(two)*

   ✳ Does each circle have the same number of triangles? *(yes)*

   ✳ Are there equal groups? *(yes)*

   ✳ How can you find out how many red triangles there are altogether? *(Answers should include the following: we could count each circle; we could repeatedly add 2 to equal the number of circles; we could multiply 2 times the number of circles.)*

   Have this group sit and have a different group stand. Repeat this style of questioning with this group. Then have the groups draw three blue squares on their circles. Ask a different group to stand and ask this group the same questions about the blue squares.

   Collect the circles and crayons from the groups and have them return to their desks.

7. Distribute the "= Equal =" worksheet to each student. Read the directions with the class. Have the students work on this individually. When all the students have finished, display the transparency and ask for volunteers to share their answers.

   Then equally share the stickers with the students in the class.

Wrap-Up

To conclude this lesson, have the students write responses using complete sentences to the following prompts in their math journal or on a sheet of notebook paper. Allow adequate time for task completion and then ask various students to share their responses with the class.

   ✳ If I said the crayons have been placed in equal groups on everyone's desk, what would that mean? *(Each desk has the same number of crayons.)*

   ✳ If you have 15 lollipops and want to share them equally among 5 friends, how could you make sure each friend gets the same number of lollipops? *(An appropriate response is as follows: I would give each friend one lollipop, then each friend another, and continue this until I shared all the lollipops.)*

Multiplication and Division *(cont.)*

Is It Equal?

Equal Groups

Jane has these bunches of roses in her garden. Each bunch has the same number of flowers.

To find out how many flowers she has in all, she can add 3 + 3 + 3 + 3. She can also multiply 3 four times (3 × 4). Jane has 12 flowers.

Are these groups equal?

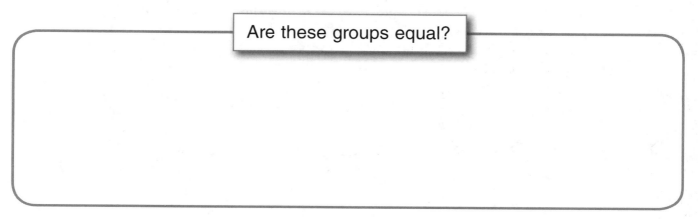

Equal Sharing

How can 18 worms be shared equally among 3 friends? Each friend can take one worm and keep doing this until all the worms are taken.

To find out how many worms each friend would get, you can subtract from 18. Keep subtracting 3 from each answer:

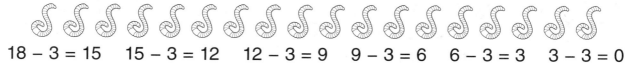

$18 - 3 = 15$ $15 - 3 = 12$ $12 - 3 = 9$ $9 - 3 = 6$ $6 - 3 = 3$ $3 - 3 = 0$

Since 3 was subtracted 6 times, each boy would get 6 worms.

You could also divide: $18 \div 3 = 6$.
Each friend would get 6 worms.

How could the 18 worms be equally shared between 2 boys?

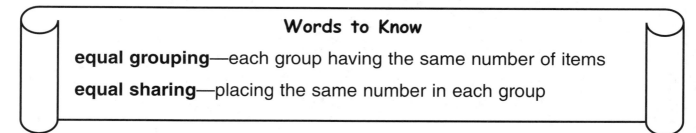

Words to Know

equal grouping—each group having the same number of items

equal sharing—placing the same number in each group

Multiplication and Division *(cont.)*

Cutouts

Multiplication and Division *(cont.)*

= Equal =

Directions: Follow each set of directions by drawing stars, bones, and candles.

1. Share 12 stars equally among the 4 papers.

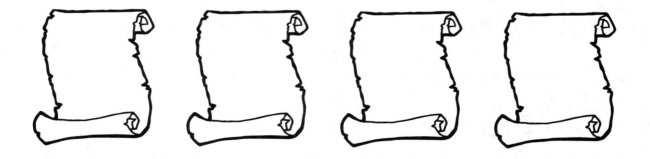

2. Share 9 bones equally among the 3 dogs.

3. Share 16 candles equally among the 4 cakes.

Illustrating Fractions

Skill 19: The student will illustrate fractions such as 1/2, 1/4, and 1/3.

Instructional Preparation

Duplicate the following (one per student, unless otherwise indicated):

- "Fractions reference sheet
- "Divide and Shade!" worksheet (*one per student pair*)
- "It's All About Fractions!" worksheet

Prepare an overhead transparency of the following:

- "Fractions" reference sheet
- "Divide and Shade!" worksheet
- "It's All About Fractions!" worksheet

Recall

Before beginning the **Review** component, facilitate a discussion based on the following questions:

✱ What is a fraction? (*part of a whole*)

✱ When do we use fractions? (*Answers will vary and may include when we talk about the amount of change we have from a dollar or describe the amount of homework finished—for example, "I have finished 1/2 of my homework."*)

Review

1. Have exactly half the students in the class stand up. Ask a volunteer to describe the students who were asked to stand using a fraction (*1/2*). Have them sit back down and explain that today they will be working with fractions.

2. Distribute the "Fractions" reference sheet and display the transparency. Review the terms and definitions in the "Words to Know" section with the class. Point out the "Remember" section just above that section. Have a student read this aloud. Tell the class that this is what they will need to remember during today's lesson.

3. Direct attention to the top of the page. Go step by step, showing the whole pie, the pie divided into four equal slices, and the pie showing one slice left. Review the parts of a fraction and how fractions are written. Have the class look at the pie that was cut into four slices. Ask the following question:

✱ How could you describe this pie as a fraction? (*4/4*)

Tell the class that when the numerator and the denominator are the same, it equals 1 whole.

Illustrating Fractions *(cont.)*

Review *(cont.)*

4. Now have the class look at the large rectangle near the center of the page. Ask for a volunteer to shade in 1/5 of the pie on the transparency. Now point out the first triangle. Show the class that it is divided into three parts. Ask the following questions:

   ✳ Is this triangle 1/3 shaded? *(no)*

   ✳ Explain your answer. *(because it is not divided into equal parts)*

   ✳ Is the second triangle 1/3 shaded? *(no)*

   ✳ Explain your answer. *(because it is not divided into equal parts)*

   ✳ Is the third triangle 1/3 shaded? *(yes)*

   ✳ How do you know? *(because it is equally divided into thirds and one of the sections is shaded)* Have the students circle the third triangle on their papers.

5. Divide the students into pairs. Display the "Divide and Shade!" transparency. Explain that for today's activity, the first pair of students will evenly divide five of the shapes and unevenly divide the other five shapes. Model dividing the rectangle into four equal sections and four unequal sections on the overhead.

   Then tell them that they will trade papers with another pair of students so that that pair can shade in the fractions for 1/2, 1/3, 1/4, 1/5, and 1/6.

6. Distribute the "Divide and Shade!" worksheet and have the pairs write their names on the first line. Then have them divide their shapes. Circulate around the room and monitor them as they divide their shapes. When the pairs have finished, have them exchange papers with another pair of students. Have them write their names on the second line of this paper. Now the pairs need to find the shapes that represent the fractions 1/2, 1/3, 1/4, 1/5, and 1/6. When they have finished, have them check their answers with the other pair. Ask for volunteers to show how they divided some of their shapes on the overhead. Have the students return to their desks.

7. Distribute the "It's All About Fractions!" worksheet. Have the students work on this paper individually. When completed, display the transparency and ask for volunteers to share their answers.

Wrap-Up

To conclude this lesson, have the students write responses using complete sentences to the following prompts in their math journal or on a sheet of notebook paper. Allow adequate time for task completion and then ask various students to share their responses with the class.

   ✳ How do you divide a shape into fourths? *(by drawing lines to make four sections of the same size)*

   ✳ If a shape is divided into six equal sections, how can you represent the fraction 1/6? *(by shading in one section)*

   ✳ When do we use fractions in daily life? *(describing the amount of cake that has been eaten or how much of a television show is left, etc.)*

Illustrating Fractions *(cont.)*

Fractions

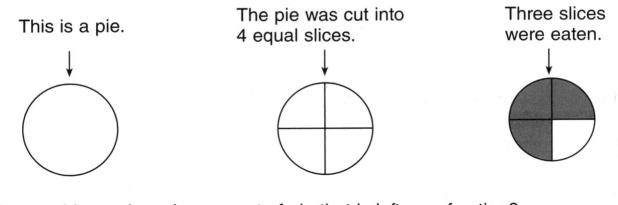

This is a pie.

The pie was cut into 4 equal slices.

Three slices were eaten.

How could you show the amount of pie that is left as a fraction?

When you write this as a fraction, you show the total number of slices there were in all, 4, on the bottom.

The number of slices that are left, 1, is the top number. $\frac{1}{4}$

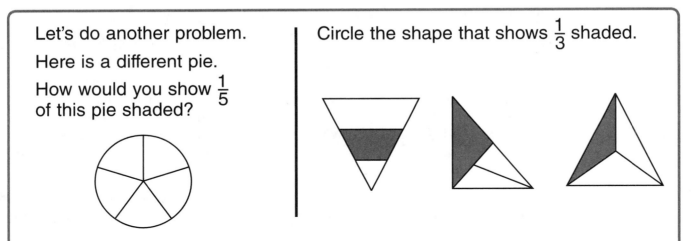

Let's do another problem.

Here is a different pie.

How would you show $\frac{1}{5}$ of this pie shaded?

Circle the shape that shows $\frac{1}{3}$ shaded.

Remember: A fractional shape is divided into equal parts.

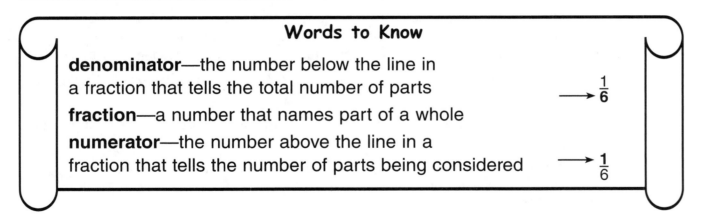

Words to Know

denominator—the number below the line in a fraction that tells the total number of parts $\longrightarrow \frac{1}{6}$

fraction—a number that names part of a whole

numerator—the number above the line in a fraction that tells the number of parts being considered $\longrightarrow \frac{1}{6}$

Illustrating Fractions *(cont.)*

Divide and Shade!

Directions for the first pair: With your partner, divide one shape into halves, one shape into thirds, one shape into fourths, one shape into fifths, and one shape into sixths. Then divide the other five shapes unevenly. Exchange papers with another pair of students.

Directions for the second pair: Find the evenly divided shapes and shade them in to show the fractions $\frac{1}{2}$, $\frac{1}{3}$, $\frac{1}{4}$, $\frac{1}{5}$, and $\frac{1}{6}$.

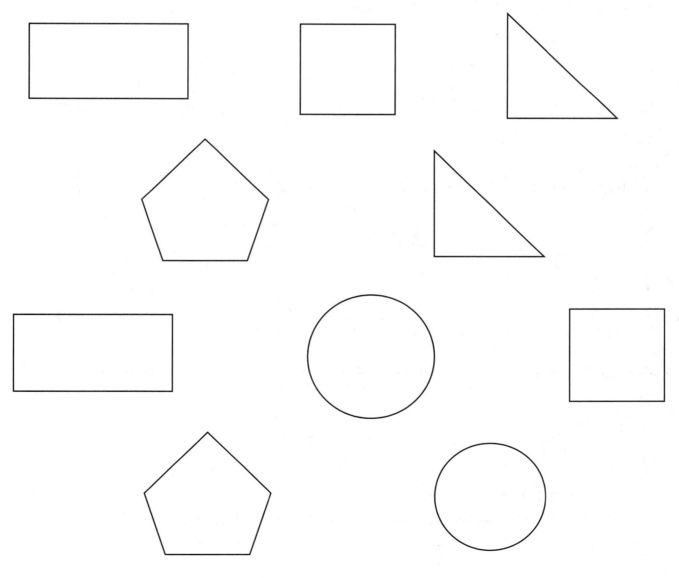

Illustrating Fractions *(cont.)*

It's All About Fractions!

1. Circle the shape that shows the fraction $\frac{1}{4}$.

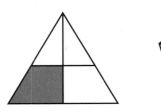 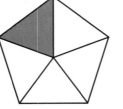 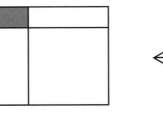 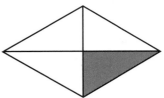

2. Shade in a shape to show the fraction $\frac{1}{6}$.

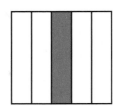 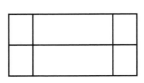 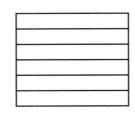 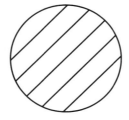

3. Draw a circle around the square that is $\frac{1}{5}$ shaded.

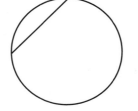 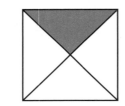 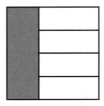 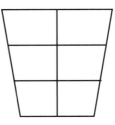

4. Shade in a shape to show the fraction $\frac{1}{2}$.

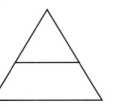 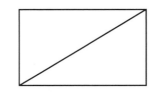 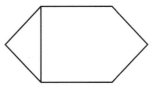

Illustrating Fractions *(cont.)*

It's All About Fractions! *(cont.)*

5. Divide this shape into fourths. Shade in $\frac{1}{4}$ of the shape.

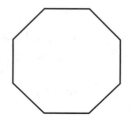

6. Divide this shape into thirds. Shade in $\frac{1}{3}$ of this shape.

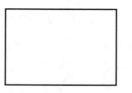

7. Shade in a shape to show the fraction $\frac{1}{4}$.

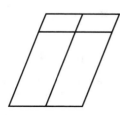 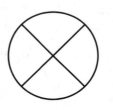 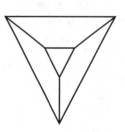

8. Draw a circle around the shape that is $\frac{1}{3}$ shaded.

 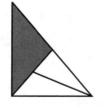  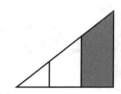

Ordering Fractions

Skill 20: The student will order the fractions 1/2, 1/4, and 1/3.

Instructional Preparation

Duplicate the following (one per student, unless otherwise indicated):

- "Fractions" reference sheet
- "What's the Order?" worksheet (*one per student pair*)
- "Least to Greatest or Greatest to Least" worksheet

Prepare an overhead transparency of the following:

- "Fractions" reference sheet
- "What's the Order?" worksheet
- "Least to Greatest or Greatest to Least" worksheet

Recall

Before beginning the **Review** component, facilitate a discussion based on these questions:

- ✳ Place these numbers in order from greatest to least: 4, 29, 92, 14. (*92, 29, 14, 4*)

- ✳ Why is it important to know how to write numbers in order from least to greatest and from greatest to least? (*Answers will vary and may include "because it's important to know if you have enough money for a purchase."*)

Review

1. Draw three circles on the board. Divide the first one into halves, the second into thirds, and the third into fourths. Tell the class to pretend that these are cookies. Shade in one section of each "cookie." Ask the following questions:

   - ✳ If I were to offer you the shaded part of these cookies, which part would you want? (*the shaded part of the first cookie*)

   - ✳ Why? (*because it is a larger piece*)

   Explain that today they are going to be placing the fractions 1/2, 1/3, and 1/4 in order.

2. Distribute the "Fractions" reference sheet and display the transparency. Review the terms and definitions in the "Words to Know" section.

3. Direct attention to the first shape on the page. As you ask the questions in the first section, write the answers on the transparency as the students write them on their paper.
   - ✳ Into how many parts is this shape divided? (*4*)
   - ✳ How many parts are shaded? (*1*)
   - ✳ What fraction of this shape is shaded? (*1/4*)

   Now have the students look at the second shape. Ask the following questions:
   - ✳ Into how many parts is this shape divided? (*2*)
   - ✳ How many parts are shaded? (*1*)
   - ✳ What fraction of this shape is shaded? (*1/2*)

Ordering Fractions *(cont.)*

Review *(cont.)*

Have the students look at the last shape. Ask the following questions:

✳ Into how many parts is this shape divided? *(3)*

✳ How many parts are shaded? *(1)*

✳ What fraction of this shape is shaded? *(1/3)*

Explain that each whole square is the same size; it is just divided into a different number of sections. Have them look carefully at each shape. Tell them you want to place the three fractions—1/2, 1/3, and 1/4—in order from the smallest fraction to the largest fraction. Ask the following questions:

✳ Which fraction represents the smallest amount of shaded space on the shape? *(1/4)* Write this fraction on the first line as the students write it on their paper.

✳ Which fraction represents the second smallest amount of shaded space on the shape? *(1/3)* Write this fraction on the second line as they write it on their paper.

✳ Which fraction represents the largest amount of shaded space on the shape? *(1/2)* Write this fraction on the third line as they write it on their paper.

Tell them that these fractions are now written in order from the smallest fraction to the largest fraction. Answer any questions they may have.

4. Place the students in pairs. Distribute the "What's the Order?" worksheet. Read the directions with the students. Remind them to look at the shaded areas in the shapes to help them decide if the fractions are in order from least to greatest or greatest to least. When the students are finished, display the transparency and ask for volunteers to share their answers. Have the students return to their seats.

5. Distribute the "Least to Greatest or Greatest to Least" worksheet. Tell them to follow the directions for each problem. They will work on this individually. When they are finished, display the transparency and review the answers as a class.

Wrap-Up

To conclude this lesson, have the students write responses using complete sentences to the following prompts in their math journal or on a sheet of notebook paper. Allow adequate time for task completion and then ask various students to share their responses with the class.

✳ What is a fraction? *(It shows a part of a whole.)*

✳ What are the parts of a fraction? *(The numerator and the denominator are the parts of a fraction.)*

✳ Why is the fraction 1/4 smaller than the fraction 1/2 when the number 4 is larger than the number 2? *(Answers may vary.)*

✳ Why is this skill important to know? *(Answers will vary and may include we use parts of a whole—such as parts of a dollar or a partially filled container—in daily life.)*

Ordering Fractions *(cont.)*

Fractions

Look at this shape.

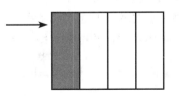

Let's describe the shaded part of this shape as a fraction.

First, write the denominator, which answers the question, "Into how many parts is this shape divided?"

Second, write the numerator, which answers the question, "How many parts are shaded?"

What fraction of this shape is shaded?

Now look at this shape.

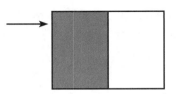

What fraction of this shape is shaded?

Both of these shapes are the same size. Which shape has the most area shaded, this one or the one at the top of the page?

That means that ½ is larger than ¼.

Now look at this shape.

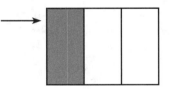

What fraction of this shape is shaded?

Use the three shapes above to help you. Write these fractions in order from the shape that has the least amount of space shaded to the shape that has the most amount of space shaded.

_____   _____   _____

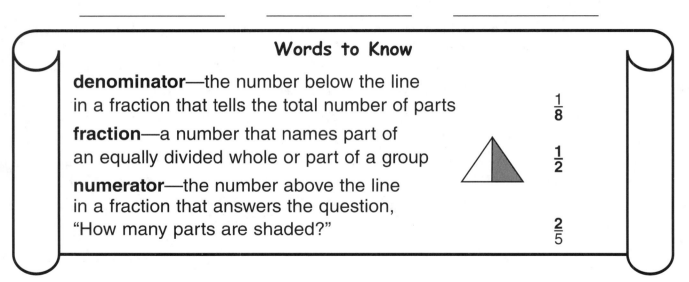

Words to Know

denominator—the number below the line in a fraction that tells the total number of parts

fraction—a number that names part of an equally divided whole or part of a group

numerator—the number above the line in a fraction that answers the question, "How many parts are shaded?"

$\frac{1}{8}$

$\frac{1}{2}$

$\frac{2}{5}$

Ordering Fractions *(cont.)*

What's the Order?

Directions: Look at each set of shapes. Write the fraction that describes the shaded part of each shape on the line below the shape. Then write on the line at the right whether the fractions you wrote are in order from "least to greatest" or "greatest to least."

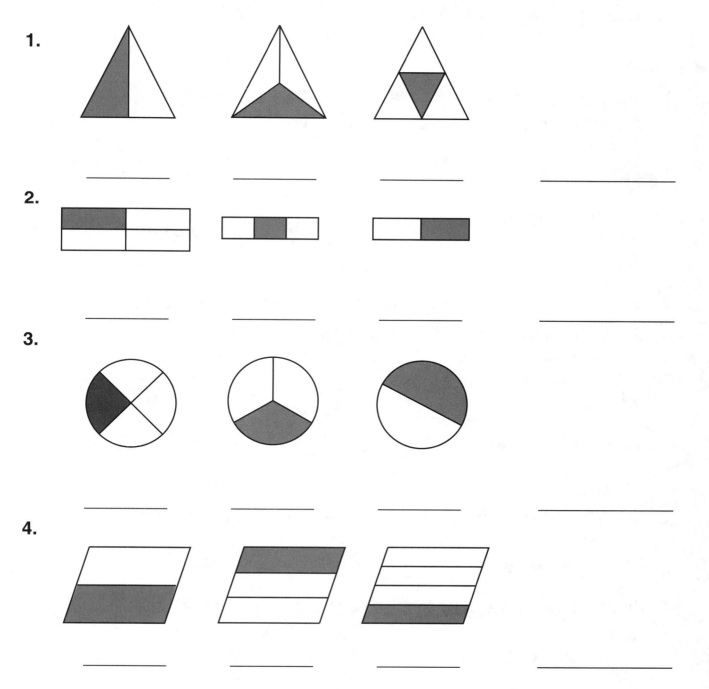

1.

_____   _____   _____   _____

2.

_____   _____   _____   _____

3.

_____   _____   _____   _____

4.

_____   _____   _____   _____

Ordering Fractions *(cont.)*

Least to Greatest or Greatest to Least

1. Write these fractions in order from least to greatest: $\frac{1}{4}, \frac{1}{2}, \frac{1}{3}$.

_____ _____ _____

2. Write these fractions in order from greatest to least: $\frac{1}{4}, \frac{1}{2}, \frac{1}{3}$.

_____ _____ _____

3. Write the fraction that describes the shaded part of each shape on the line.
Circle the order in which the shapes were placed.

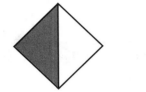 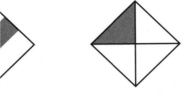

least to greatest

greatest to least

_____ _____ _____

4. Write the fraction that describes the shaded part of each shape on the line.
Circle the order in which the shapes were placed.

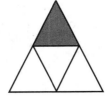 

least to greatest

greatest to least

_____ _____ _____

5. Circle the set of fractions that is in order from least to greatest.

$\frac{1}{4}, \frac{1}{2}, \frac{1}{3}$ $\frac{1}{3}, \frac{1}{4}, \frac{1}{2}$ $\frac{1}{4}, \frac{1}{3}, \frac{1}{2}$

6. Circle the set of fractions that is in order from greatest to least.

$\frac{1}{4}, \frac{1}{3}, \frac{1}{2}$ $\frac{1}{3}, \frac{1}{2}, \frac{1}{4}$ $\frac{1}{2}, \frac{1}{3}, \frac{1}{4}$

Number Words

Skill 21: The student will read number words to 100.

Instructional Preparation

Materials:

- scissors
- blank transparency sheet

Duplicate the following (one per student, unless otherwise indicated):

- "Numbers" reference sheet
- "Make the Number" cutouts (*one per student pair*)
- "Digits and Words" worksheet

Prepare an overhead transparency of the following:

- "Numbers" reference sheet
- "Digits and Words" worksheet

Recall

Before beginning the **Review** component, facilitate a discussion based on the following questions:

❋ What is a number? (*Answers will vary; accept all numbers.*)

❋ When do we use numbers? (*when counting, adding change, using the phone, etc.*)

Review

1. Ask two different students how old they are. Write these amounts using words on the board—for example, "nine" and "eight." Write these numbers vertically and add a plus sign, as if you are going to add these two amounts. Ask the class if there is a better way to write these numbers. (*yes, using digits instead of words*) Explain that sometimes it is better to use words to write numbers, and sometimes—such as when adding—it is better to use digits. Tell the class that today they will be using numbers written as digits and as words.

2. Distribute the "Numbers" reference sheet and display the transparency. Review the "Words to Know" terms and definitions with the class.

3. Read Section A with the students. Explain that it is important to know how to read and write numbers using words as well as digits. Ask the following questions:

   ❋ When would you see numbers written with digits? (*Answers will vary.*)

   ❋ When would you see numbers written using words? (*Answers will vary.*)

   Review the numbers 0 through 19, showing the pattern created by the digits and the way they are written as words. Ask for a volunteer to read the numbers 0 through 19 as the class follows along.

Number Words *(cont.)*

Review *(cont.)*

4. Have the students look at Section B. Read the steps needed to write the number words to the class. Have the class count by tens from ten to ninety aloud. Explain that these are the words they write first when they write the number words. Review each of the numbers with the class, pointing out how the steps are being followed—first by writing the word that was said when counting by tens, then the hyphen, and then the number in the ones place. Ask the class for help writing the number words for the numbers *41* and *29*. Write these words on the lines provided on the transparency. (*forty-one, twenty-nine*)

   Ask a student to read the "Remember" section. Explain that these are the numbers over 20 that you do not say when you count by tens.

5. Place the students in pairs and distribute the "Make the Number" cutout page. Have the students cut out the numbers and the hyphen. When they have the numbers cut out, have them place all the numbers they say when they count by tens on the table with the partner on the left, and the rest of the numbers on the table with the partner on the right. Write the following numbers one by one on a blank transparency: *96, 32, 55, 82, 40, 69, 74, 21, 18, 11*, and *6*. Have each pair make the number on the table. Walk around the room to see if each pair has made the number correctly. If there is a pair that did not do it correctly, write it on the transparency correctly. Continue writing each number and monitoring the students for accuracy. Do additional numbers, if necessary.

   Now write the number *100*. Ask the class how they think that number would be written. Write the correct way on the transparency, showing the class that a hyphen is not used.

6. Distribute the "Digits and Words" worksheet and display the transparency. Read the directions with the class. Have the students work on this individually. When completed, review the answers as a class.

Wrap-Up

To conclude this lesson, have the students write responses using complete sentences to the following prompts in their math journal or on a sheet of notebook paper. Allow adequate time for task completion and then ask various students to share their responses with the class.

* What is a digit? (*any one of ten symbols used to write numbers: 0, 1, 2, 3, 4, 5, 6, 7, 8, and 9*)

* What is a number word? Give an example. (*A number word is a number written as a word, such as "eight."*)

* When do you use a hyphen? (*You use a hyphen when the number word is over twenty and the number in the ones place is not zero.*)

* Why is it important to know how to read numbers using both digits and words? (*The numbers could be written either way, and you need to be able to understand them.*)

Number Words *(cont.)*

Numbers

Section A

There are two different ways to write a number: you can use digits *or* you can use words. For example, the number *18* can also be written as the word *eighteen.*

Writing numbers using words follows a pattern,

0	1	2	3	4	5	6	7	8	9
zero	one	two	three	four	five	six	seven	eight	nine
10	11	12	13	14	15	16	17	18	19
ten	eleven	twelve	thirteen	fourteen	fifteen	sixteen	seventeen	eighteen	nineteen

Section B

Here is how to write numbers over 20:

- **First,** you write the number as if you were counting by 10s.
- **Next,** you add a hyphen. Then you write the word from the ones

25 = twenty-five	62 = sixty-two
31 = thirty-one	73 = seventy-three
44 = forty-four	86 = eighty-six
58 = fifty-eight	97 = ninety-seven
41 = _____	29 = _____

Remember: Use a hyphen when the number is over twenty and the number in the ones place is not zero.

Words to Know

digit—Any one of ten symbols used to write numbers   *0, 1, 2, 3, 4, 5, 6, 7, 8, 9*

hyphen—used to separate two number words

number word—a number written as a word.   *nine*

Number Words *(cont.)*

Make the Number

zero	one	two	three	four
five	six	seven	eight	nine
ten	eleven	twelve	thirteen	fourteen
fifteen	sixteen	seventeen	eighteen	nineteen
twenty	thirty	forty	fifty	sixty
seventy	eighty	ninety	one hundred	—

Name: _____

Number Words *(cont.)*

Digits and Words

Directions: Write the number shown using digits.

1. seventy-four _____

2. thirty-one _____

3. eighty _____

4. twenty-five _____

5. eleven _____

6. sixty-three _____

7. ninety-six _____

8. forty-eight _____

9. fifty-seven _____

10. fourteen _____

Directions: Draw lines matching the numbers.

seventeen   (13)

ninety-one   (17)

seventy   (7)

eighty-four   (52)

seven   (70)

thirteen   (91)

thirty-nine   (84)

fifty-two   (39)

Number Lines

Skill 22: The student will read, write, compare, and order numbers on a number line.

Instructional Preparation

Materials:

- a container with different pieces of paper showing these amounts: 3,490; 3,450; 4,200; and 4,390

Duplicate the following (one per student, unless otherwise indicated):

- "Number Lines" reference sheet
- "Plot, Compare, and Order" worksheet (*one per student pair*)
- "Number Lines Are Fun!" worksheet

Prepare an overhead transparency of the following:

- "Number Lines" reference sheet
- "Plot, Compare, and Order" worksheet
- "Number Lines Are Fun!" worksheet

Recall

Before beginning the **Review** component, facilitate a discussion based on the following questions:

 ✳ When do we use numbers? (*Answers will vary.*)

 ✳ Why is it important to know which numbers are larger or smaller than other numbers? (*Answer will vary.*)

Review

1. Reach into the container and take out two numbers. Ask the class which number is the larger number. Take out another number and ask if anyone knows an easy way to place these numbers in order from smallest to largest. Explain that today they are going to use a number line, which will help them compare and order numbers.

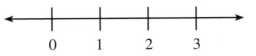

2. Distribute the "Number Lines" reference sheet and display the transparency. Review the meaning of a number line in the "Words to Know" section.

Review *(cont.)*

3. Direct attention to the number line at the top of the page. Remind the students that number lines are shown with arrows at each end, indicating that the line continues in both directions. Tell the class that each number line they will use will show a different set of numbers, which means a different part of the number line is being shown. Point out how the numbers increase as they go to the right. Ask the following questions:

    ✳ What would be the next number on this number line? (*30*)

    ✳ How do you know? (*because the numbers are increasing by one, and 30 comes after 29*)

    ✳ If we continued the number line to the left, what would the next number be? (*22*)

    ✳ How do you know? (*because 22 is one less than 23*)

4. Now look at the "Plotting Numbers" section. Ask the following questions:

    ✳ What range of numbers is shown on this number line? (*the numbers 34 through 48*)

    ✳ How do you know this is the range? (*The first number shown is 34, and the last number shown is 48.*)

    Besides showing different numbers, what else about this number line is different from the top one we looked at? (*The numbers go up by twos.*)

    Instead of all the numbers being shown, two of the numbers are represented by letters. Ask the following questions:

    ✳ Look at the letter A. How can we find out what number the letter A represents? (*by counting by twos*)

    ✳ What number does the A represent? (*42*)

    Write the number underneath the dot on the transparency and have the students write the number on their paper. Follow the same line of questioning for the letter B. (*46*)

5. Direct attention to the next section, "Comparing Numbers." Tell the class that number lines can help them when they want to compare different numbers. Have the students place their pencil point on the number 84. Check to make sure all the students have found this number, and then tell the class they need to find out which number is 5 less than 84. Show the class how to count back 5 numbers to get the answer, 79. Ask the following questions:

    ✳ How can you find out which number is 3 more than 78? (*Place your pencil on the 78 and count up 3 numbers*)

    ✳ Which way do you go on a number line to get a larger number? (*to the right*)

    Ask for a few volunteers to ask similar questions for the class to solve using this number line.

Review *(cont.)*

6. Have the class look at the last section, "Ordering Numbers." Tell the students that number lines can help them when they need to order numbers. Tell them that they need to place these numbers in order from smallest to largest: *325, 275,* and *350.* Write these numbers on the board for the students to see and then ask the following question:

   How can you use a number line to order these numbers from least to greatest? *(Answers should include knowing that a number line increases as it goes to the right, so the first number on the number line is 275, the second is 325, and the third is 350.)*

   Now tell the class that you want to place 300, 450, and 400 in order from largest to smallest. Write these numbers on the board and ask the following questions:

   * Can this number line help you place these numbers in order? *(yes)*

   * How can it help you when some of the numbers are not shown? *(Answers will vary but should include that you can find the missing numbers by counting by 25s, and then you can order the numbers.)*

   * What is the correct order of these numbers from greatest to least? *(450, 400, 300)*

   * Did the number line help you order the numbers? *(Answers will vary.)*

   On the board, draw a number line showing numbers in the thousands. Here is an example:

   | 3,343 | 3,346 | 3,349 | 3,352 | 3,355 | E | 3,361 | 3,364 | 3,367 | 3,370 |

   Ask questions similar to the ones above, finding the missing number and ordering a few of these numbers from least to greatest and greatest to least. Explain to the class that number lines can be helpful when dealing with larger numbers.

7. Place the students into pairs. Distribute the "Plot, Compare, and Order" worksheet and display its transparency. Read the directions with the class, answering any questions they may have. Monitor the students by circulating around the room and observing how they are solving each problem. When the class has finished this activity, ask for volunteers to share their answers. Have the students return to their desks.

   Distribute the "Number Lines Are Fun!" worksheet. Read the directions with the class and have the students work on this independently. When they have finished, display the transparency and ask for volunteers to share their answers.

Wrap-Up

To conclude this lesson, have the students write responses using complete sentences to the following prompts in their math journal or on a sheet of notebook paper. Allow adequate time for task completion and then ask various students to share their responses with the class.

   * What can a number line help you do? *(order and compare numbers)*

   * Where do you see a number line in daily life? *(Answers will vary.)*

Number Lines (cont.)

Reference Sheet

23   24   25   26   27   28   29

Plotting Numbers

A   B

34   36   38   40   44   48

Comparing Numbers

77   78   79   80   81   82   83   84   85

Ordering Numbers

C   D

275   325   350   375   425   450

Name: _____

Number Lines *(cont.)*

Plot, Compare, and Order

Directions: First, plot the missing numbers on the number line. Then, compare the numbers and write the answer on the line. Finally, order the numbers using the number line.

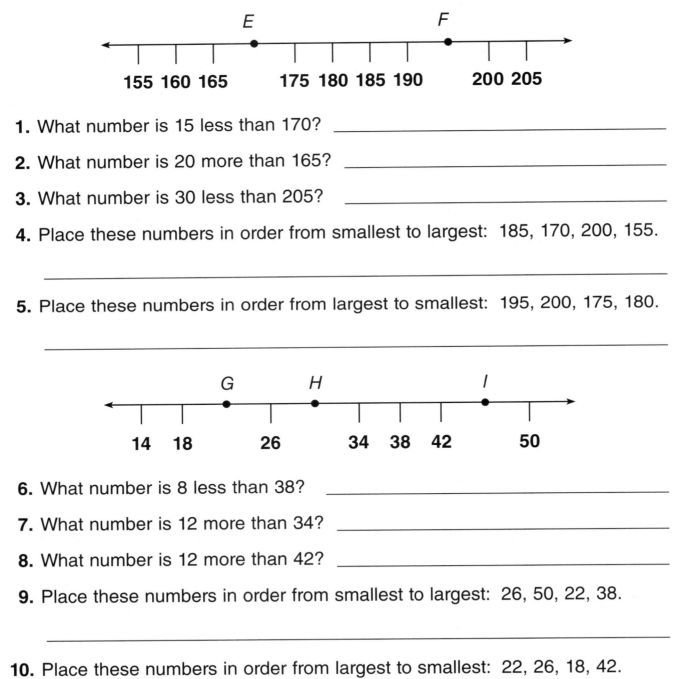

1. What number is 15 less than 170? _____

2. What number is 20 more than 165? _____

3. What number is 30 less than 205? _____

4. Place these numbers in order from smallest to largest: 185, 170, 200, 155.

_____

5. Place these numbers in order from largest to smallest: 195, 200, 175, 180.

_____

6. What number is 8 less than 38? _____

7. What number is 12 more than 34? _____

8. What number is 12 more than 42? _____

9. Place these numbers in order from smallest to largest: 26, 50, 22, 38.

_____

10. Place these numbers in order from largest to smallest: 22, 26, 18, 42.

_____

Number Lines (cont.)

Number Lines Are Fun!

Directions: Answer the questions using the number line shown.

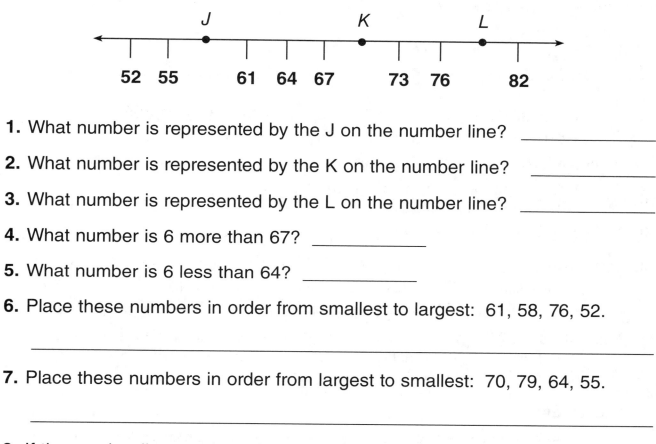

1. What number is represented by the J on the number line? _____

2. What number is represented by the K on the number line? _____

3. What number is represented by the L on the number line? _____

4. What number is 6 more than 67? _____

5. What number is 6 less than 64? _____

6. Place these numbers in order from smallest to largest: 61, 58, 76, 52.

   _____

7. Place these numbers in order from largest to smallest: 70, 79, 64, 55.

   _____

8. If the number line continued to the right, what number would be next?

   _____

9. Fill in the circle of the number you counted by to find the missing numbers on this number line.

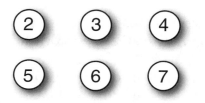

Rote Counting

Skill 23: The student will rote count to 100 beginning with any number.

Instructional Preparation

Materials:

- pencil jar containing pencils
- "Cutouts" pages cut into sets
- blank transparency sheet

Duplicate the following (one per student, unless otherwise indicated):

- "Say It in Order" reference sheet
- "The Order Is . . ." worksheet
- "The Next Numbers Are . . ." worksheet

Prepare an overhead transparency of the following:

- "Say It in Order" reference sheet
- "The Order Is . . ." worksheet
- "The Next Numbers Are . . ." worksheet

Recall

Before beginning the **Review** component, facilitate a discussion based on these questions:

* ✳ How can you find out how many pencils are in the jar? (*Answer should include "counting them."*)

* ✳ How would you count them? (*Start with one and count until all the pencils have been counted.*)

Review

1. Ask one of the students in class how old he or she is. Ask the student to tell you which birthdays he or she has had so far, starting with the first one. Explain to the class that today they are going to count by ones starting with different numbers.

2. Distribute the "Say It in Order" reference sheet and display the transparency. Review the terms and definitions in the "Words to Know" section with the class. Give a few different numbers as examples, having the class tell you the digit in the ones column and the digit in the tens column.

3. Direct the students' attention to the top of the page. Have the class count aloud to 20. Write the numbers they say on the lines provided. (*4, 5, 6, 7, 8, 9, 10, 11, 12, 13, 14, 15, 16, 17, 18, 19, 20*) Have the students write these numbers on their paper. Tell the class that this time they will be counting to 20; however, they will not be starting with the number 1. Explain that the first three numbers—11, 12, and 13—have been given for them. Remind the class that when counting, they need to use their place value. The number in the ones column continues to increase until the digit is 9, then the number in the tens column will change. Count as a class and have the students fill in the numbers on their paper as you say them together. (*14, 15, 16, 17, 18, 19, 20*)

Rote Counting *(cont.)*

Review *(cont.)*

4. Ask the following questions:

  ✳ Did the order of the numbers change? *(no)*

  ✳ Did you say the same numbers? *(yes, from 11 on up)*

  Remind the class that it does not matter where you start counting from, the order of the numbers does not change. Write the following numbers on a blank transparency and ask for different volunteers to tell you the three numbers that come next. Tell the class to pay attention to the place value of the digits in order to decide which number comes next in the set.

  19, 20, 21, _____ *(22, 23, 24)*

  43, 44, 45, _____ *(46, 47, 48)*

  58, 59, _____ *(60, 61, 62)*

5. Read the "Think About It" question with the class. Give them time to think about their answers and ask for volunteers to share their ideas. *(adding money to an existing amount, counting how many more baseball cards you have when given extra, etc.)*

6. Place the students in pairs. Give each pair one card from the "Cutouts" pages. Distribute copies of "The Order Is . . ." worksheet. Have them write in the squares in Row A the numbers on the card in order from the smallest value to the largest value. Then have them write the three numbers that would come next on the lines. When they have finished, they need to raise their hands for you to check for accuracy. Have them exchange cards with a different pair and write the numbers on this card on the next row of the worksheet. Continue this process until the worksheet has been completed. Circulate around the room to monitor progress and to answer any questions the students may have. When they have completed the worksheet, ask for volunteers to share the numbers they received, the order they placed them in, and the numbers they wrote on their paper.

7. Distribute "The Next Numbers Are . . ." worksheet and display the transparency. Read the directions with the class. Have them work on this independently. When the students have finished, ask for volunteers to share their answers and write them on the transparency.

Wrap-Up

To conclude this lesson, have the students write responses using complete sentences to the following prompts in their math journal or on a sheet of notebook paper. Allow adequate time for task completion and then ask various students to share their responses with the class.

  ✳ What do you need to pay attention to in order to count by ones? *(place value, the number in the ones place, and the number in the tens place)*

  ✳ When would you count in daily life? *(Answers will vary and may include counting the number of pages you have left to read or counting how many times you can jump rope without missing.)*

Rote Counting *(cont.)*

Say It in Order

Let's count to 20.

1, 2, 3, ____, ____, ____, ____, ____, ____, ____, ____, ____, ____,

____, ____, ____, ____, ____, ____, ____,

Now let's count to 20, starting with 11.

11, 12, 13, ____, ____, ____, ____, ____, ____, ____

Did the order of the numbers change? _____

Did you say the same numbers? _____

Starting with a number other than 1 *does not* change the order of the numbers you say.

Think About It

When would you count starting with a number other than 1?

Words to Know

ones place—the number in the ones column. ⟶ 23

place value—the value of a digit's place in a number.   *234 = 2 hundreds, 3 tens, and 4 ones*

tens place—the number in the tens column ⟶ 84

Rote Counting *(cont.)*

Cutouts

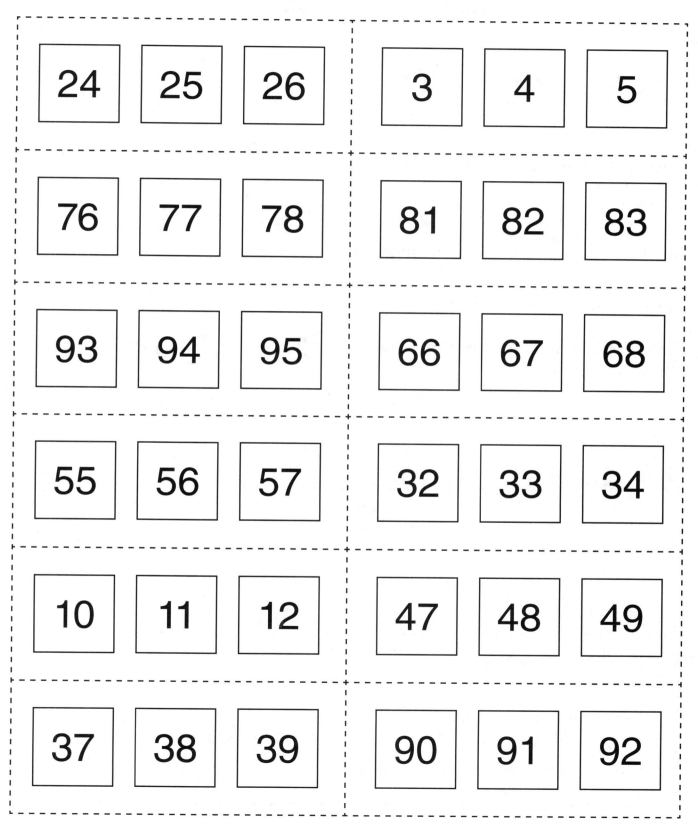

24	25	26		3	4	5
76	77	78		81	82	83
93	94	95		66	67	68
55	56	57		32	33	34
10	11	12		47	48	49
37	38	39		90	91	92

Rote Counting (cont.)

Cutouts (cont.)

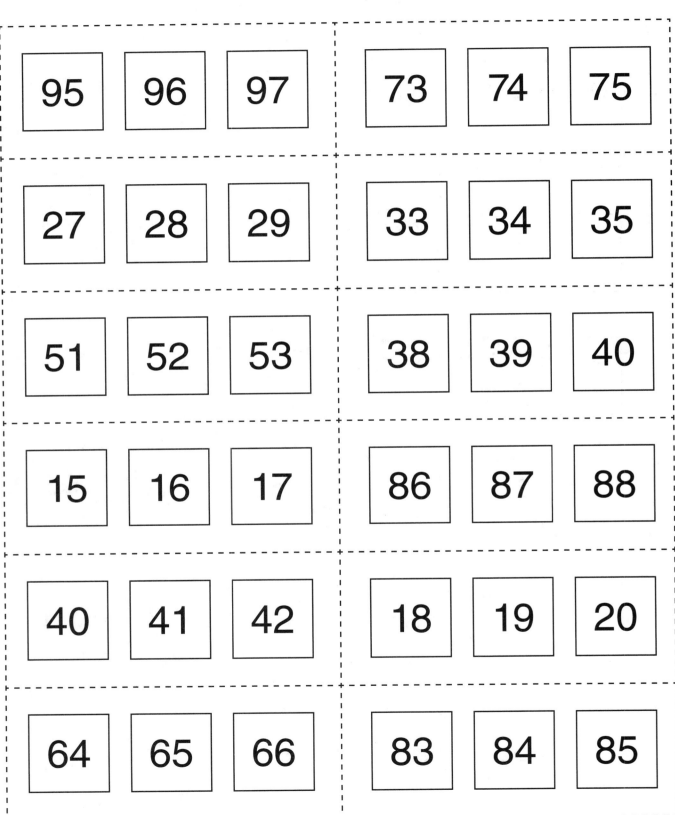

95	96	97		73	74	75
27	28	29		33	34	35
51	52	53		38	39	40
15	16	17		86	87	88
40	41	42		18	19	20
64	65	66		83	84	85

Name: _____ #6213 ES: Math

Rote Counting (cont.)

The Order Is . . .

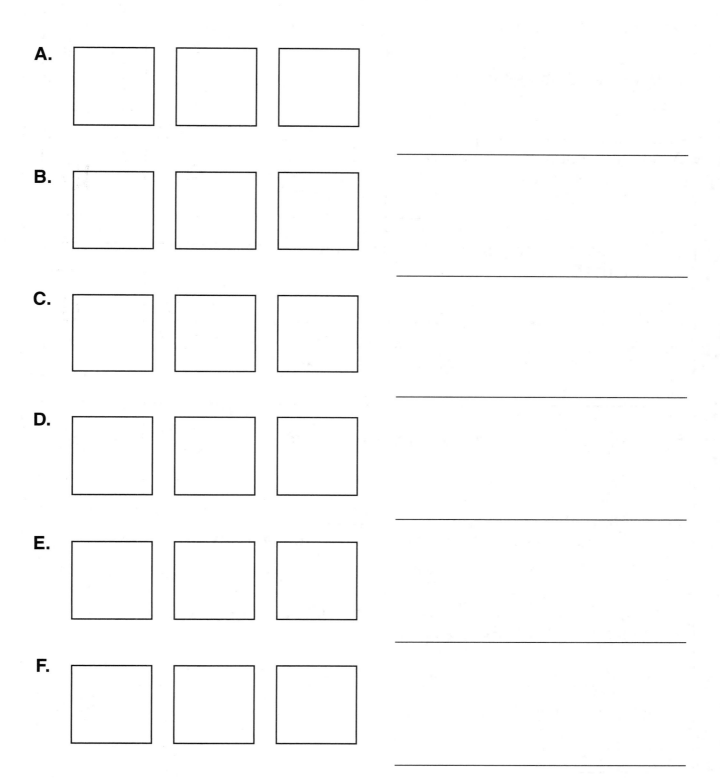

Name: _____

Rote Counting *(cont.)*

The Next Numbers Are . . .

Directions: Write the answer for each question on the lines provided.

---

1. Write the numbers that come next.

88, 89, 90, 91, _____, _____, _____, _____

---

2. Marla is counting her marbles. She just said 78 and 79. What numbers will she say next?

_____, _____, _____

---

3. Zack just read pages 92, 93, and 94 in his book. Which pages will Zack read next?

_____, _____, _____, _____

---

4. Sarah is "it" in a game of hide-and-seek. She just said the numbers 44 and 45. What numbers will Sarah say next?

_____, _____, _____, _____

---

5. Write the numbers that come next when you are counting by ones.

68, 69, _____, _____, _____, _____

---

6. Frank is counting the cars as they go by. He just said 49, 50, and 51. Which numbers will Frank say as the next group of cars goes by?

_____, _____, _____

---

7. Betty is counting the seconds on her clock. She just said 20 and 21. What numbers will Betty say next?

_____, _____, _____, _____

---

8. Write the numbers that come next.

71, 72, _____, _____, _____

Equivalent Forms

Skill 24: The student will show equivalent forms of the same number (up to 20).

Instructional Preparation

Materials:

- sheet of paper (*one per group*)
- pencil (*one per group*)

Duplicate the following (one per student, unless otherwise indicated):

- "Equal Sums" reference sheet
- "Write It Differently!" worksheet

Prepare an overhead transparency of the following:

- "Equal Sums" reference sheet
- "Write It Differently!" worksheet

Recall

Before beginning the **Review** component, facilitate a discussion based on the following questions:

- ✳ If Sam and I each check out four books from the library, how can you describe the numbers of books? (*Answers will vary but may include each having the same or an equal amount.*)

- ✳ Two of my books are mysteries and two are funny. All four of Sam's books are about baseball. Can the number of books we each have be described differently using numbers? (*Yes, your books are 2 + 2. They still equal 4 books.*)

Review

1. Group five boys together and five girls together in the front of the classroom. Ask the following questions:

   - ✳ How can these students be described? (*5 boys and 5 girls*)

   - ✳ How can I write this as a number sentence? (*The answer 5 + 5 may be given; if so, emphasize that both sides are equal, showing 5 = 5.*)

   Tell the students that they are correct; however, there are different ways these numbers can be written and still be equal. Separate the girls into groups of two and three. Show the class that two girls plus three girls still equals five girls, which also equals the number of boys. The number of girls didn't change—just the way they were grouped changed. Explain to the students that today they are going to group numbers in different ways, without changing the value.

Review *(cont.)*

2. Display the "Words to Know" section on the "Equal Numbers" reference sheet. Review the terms and definitions with the class. Distribute the "Equal Numbers" reference sheet and explain that the sum *8* is shown on this page in different ways. Show the class that in the first section the sum 8 is written as different addition problems involving two numbers. The next section shows how adding an equal sign and the number *8*—making both sides have the same value—can make a number sentence. Tell the class that you can add more than two numbers together to equal 8, as shown in the third section. Ask volunteers to give some other examples of ways to make the sum *8*, and write these answers on the transparency while the students write them on the lines.

   Direct attention to the rounded rectangle. Ask the following questions:

   ✳ How is the sum *8* being shown in this section? (*using subtraction*)

   ✳ Can subtraction be used to show the sum *8*? Why or why not? (*yes, because both sides of the equal sign have the same value*)

   Ask for different examples of using subtraction to represent the sum *8* and write these on the transparency. Have the students write them on the lines on their reference sheet.

3. Place the students into groups of three or four with one sheet of paper and a pencil. Tell them that you will be writing a number on the board, and each group needs to write five different equivalent forms of the number on the paper. Encourage them to use combinations of two or more numbers and subtraction problems. Give an adequate amount of time for the students to complete their task. Ask for an equivalent form from each group and write these under the number. If the class agrees that all forms are equivalent to the number on the board, erase the board and write a different number. Continue this activity using numbers up to 20 and begin setting a time limit for the groups to write their equivalent forms.

4. Distribute the "Write It Differently!" worksheet and display the transparency. Read the directions for the first section and have the students work on this individually. When they have finished, read the directions for the second section. Have the students work on this section individually, as well. Circulate around the room to monitor understanding. When the class has finished, ask for volunteers to share their answers, and write them on the transparency. Ask for a few students to share their different answers for each of the problems in the second section.

Wrap-Up

To conclude this lesson, have the students write a response using complete sentences to the following prompts in their math journal or on a sheet of notebook paper. Allow adequate time for task completion and then ask various students to share their responses with the class.

   ✳ Write some different ways the sum *18* can be shown. (*10 + 8, 9 + 9, etc.*)

   ✳ When can you use this skill in daily life? (*Answers will vary. They may include in purchasing items at a store, measuring, or finding a sum or a difference.*)

Equivalent Forms *(cont.)*

Equal Sums

Look at the number *8*. It's sum can be written in many ways.

1 + 7	7 + 1
2 + 6	6 + 2
3 + 5	5 + 3
4 + 4	

Here these sums are written as equations.

1 + 7 = 8	7 + 1 = 8
2 + 6 = 8	6 + 2 = 8
3 + 5 = 8	5 + 3 = 8

A sum can also be written using more than two numbers.

3 + 2 + 3 = 8   5 + 2 + 1 = 8

What are some other ways you can write an equivalent form of the sum *8*?

_____   _____

_____   _____

You can also use subtraction to show equivalent forms of a sum.

20 – 12 = 8   10 – 2 = 8

How else could you write an equivalent form of the number 8 using subtraction?

_____   _____

_____   _____

Words to Know

equal—having the same amount

equation—a number sentence with an equal sign to show that two amounts are equal

number sentence—a sentence that shows numbers on both sides of the equal sign having the same value

Name: _____

Equivalent Forms *(cont.)*

Write It Differently!

Directions: Draw a line connecting the different forms of the same sum.

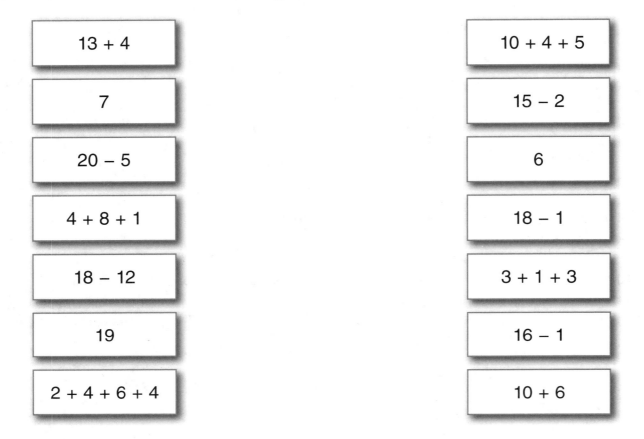

13 + 4	10 + 4 + 5
7	15 – 2
20 – 5	6
4 + 8 + 1	18 – 1
18 – 12	3 + 1 + 3
19	16 – 1
2 + 4 + 6 + 4	10 + 6

Directions: Write an equivalent form for each sum.

1. 7 _____

2. 8 – 3 _____

3. 12 + 2 + 4 _____

4. 2 + 4 + 5 + 1 + 2 _____

5. 11 – 5 _____

6. 16 _____

Place Value and Expanded Notation

Skill 25: The student will write and apply whole numbers using place value and expanded notation to 100.

Instructional Preparation

Duplicate and prepare an overhead transparency of the following:
- "What's the Value?" reference sheet
- "It's Expanded!" worksheet (*one per pair*)

Recall

Before beginning the **Review** component, facilitate a discussion based on these questions:

- ✳ What are some examples of whole numbers? (*Answers will vary.*)
- ✳ When do we use numbers in our day-to-day lives? (*Answers will vary.*)

Review

1. Ask a volunteer to count the students in class. Have him or her write this total on the board. Tell the class that today they will be writing this number in different ways. Explain that they are going to use place value and expanded notation.

2. Distribute and display the "What's the Value?" reference sheet. Review the "Words to Know" terms and definitions with the class.

3. Ask for a volunteer to read the top section of the "What's the Value?" page to the class. Remind the students that if they know place value, writing or reading a number in expanded notation is easy. Go step by step over the rest of the page. Tell the class that numbers can also be described by saying the digit in each place value. Ask the class:

   ✳ How can 8 tens and 4 ones be shown two different ways? (*84 and 80 + 4*)

   Direct attention to the "Challenge" section. Ask if anyone has an idea how to write the "20" in expanded notation. Explain that since the digit in the ones column is a zero, it is used only as a placeholder in the number. So, when this number is written in expanded form, the zero is left out; we just write "20." Explain that when we see a number written using just the digits, such as "15," this is called *standard form*. Direct attention to the number of students in the class. Ask a volunteer to write this number on the board using place value and expanded notation.

4. Place the students in pairs. Distribute the "It's Expanded!" worksheet to each pair. Review the directions with the class and monitor them as they work on this activity. When the students have finished, display the transparency and review their answers. (*1. Y; 2. M; 3. S; 4. B; 5. F; 6. K; 7. A; 8. T; 9. R; 10. V; 40 + 5; 80 + 9; and 70 + 2*)

Wrap-Up

To conclude this lesson, have the students write responses using complete sentences to the following prompts in their math journal or on a sheet of notebook paper.

- ✳ Write the number ninety-six in standard form, expanded notation, and using place value. (*96, 90 + 6, and 9 tens, 6 ones*)
- ✳ Why do you think it is important to know how to write a number using expanded notation? (*Answers will vary.*)

Place Value and Expanded Notation *(cont.)*

What's the Value?

Our number system is based on tens. We use the digits 0–9 to describe the value of a number. Where these digits are placed tells us the value of the number.

This number tells us there are 8 digits in the ones column.   ⟶   **8**

Let's add 20 to this number.   ⟶   **28**

When we write this number in expanded notation,   ⟶   **20 + 8 = 28** we write each digit's value.

Show two ways to write 8 tens and 4 ones.

_____

_____

Challenge

Write 20 in expanded notation.

_____

Words to Know

expanded notation—a way to write numbers that shows the place value of each digit

78 = 70 + 8

place value—the value of a digit in a number

There are 7 tens and 8 ones in the number 78.

Place Value and Expanded Notation *(cont.)*

It's Expanded!

Directions: On the line, write the letter of the number, place value, or expanded notation that has the same value as the problem. The first one has been done for you.

1. 34	_____Y_____	
2. 47	_____	
3. 38	_____	
4. 77	_____	
5. 51	_____	
6. 99	_____	
7. 30 + 2	_____	
8. 40 + 3	_____	
9. 10 + 1	_____	
10. 60 + 4	_____	

A	32	**N**	5 ones, 1 ten
B	70 + 7	**O**	403
C	302	**P**	10 + 7
D	8 tens, 3 ones	**Q**	50 + 10
E	90 + 1	**R**	1 ten, 1 one
F	5 tens, 1 one	**S**	3 tens, 8 ones
G	23	**T**	43
H	77 + 7	**U**	101
I	4 + 70	**V**	6 tens, 4 ones
J	6 ones, 4 tens	**W**	3 ones, 4 tens
K	9 tens, 9 ones	**X**	90 + 90
L	604	**Y**	30 + 4
M	40 + 7	**Z**	3 + 4

Directions: On the lines provided, write each number in expanded notation.

45 _____

89 _____

72 _____

Repeated Addition

Skill 26: The student will apply repeated addition to problem-solving situations.

Instructional Preparation

Duplicate the following (one per student, unless otherwise indicated):

- "Repeated Addition" reference sheet
- "Match It, Write It, Solve It!" worksheet (*one per student pair*)
- "Write, Then Solve!" worksheet

Prepare an overhead transparency of the following:

- "Repeated Addition" reference sheet
- "Match It, Write It, Solve It!" worksheet
- "Write, Then Solve!" worksheet

Recall

Before beginning the **Review** component, facilitate a discussion based on the following questions:

　✳ When a question asks you to find the total number of something, or how many in all, what kind of problem are you solving? (*addition*)

　✳ Give an example of a story problem that you need to use addition to solve. (*Answers will vary. Accept appropriate responses. Example: James has four black T-shirts and three white T-shirts. How many T-shirts does James have in all?*)

Review

1. Tell the class you want to give two sheets of paper to each girl in the class that has brown hair. Ask the class the following question:

　✳ How can I find out how many pieces of paper I will need? (*Answers will vary and may include counting each girl and doubling the answer or skip counting by 2s.*)

   Explain that today they are going to use repeated addition to find the answers to these types of questions.

2. Distribute the "Repeated Addition" reference sheet and display the transparency. Review the terms and definitions in the "Words to Know" section with the class.

Review *(cont.)*

3. Direct attention to the top of the page. Discuss each section of the worksheet with the class. Remind them that using repeated addition is very helpful in solving problems in which the same number is being used. Tell the class that after the problem has been set up, skip counting is one way to find the total.

    Now pose the following problem to the class: "Pete bought 8 pencils. He spent 4 cents for each pencil. How much money did Pete spend in all?" Ask the following questions and write the responses on a blank transparency:

    ✳ How much did each pencil cost? (*4 cents*)

    ✳ How many pencils did Pete buy? (*8 pencils*)

    ✳ How can we use repeated addition to find out how much money Pete spent? (*4 + 4 + 4 + 4 + 4 + 4 + 4 + 4 or 8 + 8 + 8 + 8*)

    ✳ What could you do to help find the answer? (*Skip count by 4s: 4, 8, 12, 16, 20, 24, 28, 32; or skip count by 8s: 8, 16, 24, 32.*)

    ✳ How much did Pete spend on pencils? (*32 cents*)

    If you feel it is necessary, ask the class another set of questions, using the above format but with marbles that cost three cents each.

4. Place the students in pairs. Distribute the "Match It, Write It, Solve It!" worksheet and display the transparency. Read the directions with the class. Circulate around the room to monitor student progress. When the students are finished, ask for volunteers to share which repeated-addition problem they chose to fit each of the problems and draw the line on the transparency. Then review the answers for A and B, having two volunteers write their answers on the transparency. Be sure to point out both ways each could be written. Have the students return to their desks.

5. Distribute the "Write, Then Solve!" worksheet and display the transparency. Read the directions with the class. Ask the class to answer the questions in complete sentences, since this will help to ensure they understand the correct way to apply the repeated addition. Have the students work on this individually. When completed, review the answers as a class.

Wrap-Up

To conclude this lesson, have the students write responses using complete sentences to the following prompts in their math journal or on a sheet of notebook paper. Allow adequate time for task completion and then ask various students to share their responses with the class.

    ✳ How can using repeated addition help you solve a problem? (*Answers will vary.*)

    ✳ When can using this skill help you in everyday life? (*Answers will vary.*)

Repeated Addition *(cont.)*

Reference Sheet

Jerry wants to count the worth of his nickels.

- He has five nickels.

- He knows that each nickel is worth 5 cents.

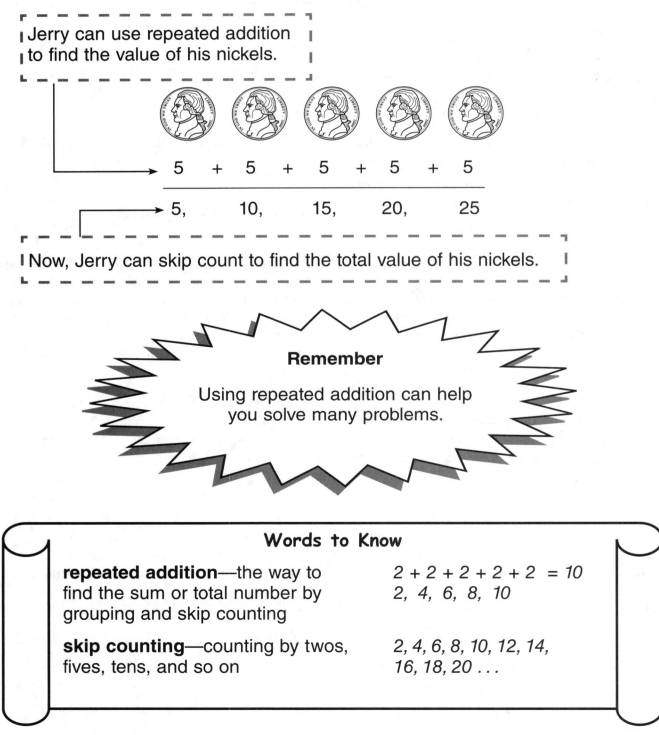

Jerry can use repeated addition to find the value of his nickels.

5 + 5 + 5 + 5 + 5

5,   10,   15,   20,   25

Now, Jerry can skip count to find the total value of his nickels.

Remember

Using repeated addition can help you solve many problems.

Words to Know	
repeated addition—the way to find the sum or total number by grouping and skip counting	$2 + 2 + 2 + 2 + 2 = 10$ *2, 4, 6, 8, 10*
skip counting—counting by twos, fives, tens, and so on	*2, 4, 6, 8, 10, 12, 14,* *16, 18, 20 . . .*

Repeated Addition (cont.)

Match It, Write It, Solve It!

Directions: Draw a line from each problem to the repeated addition that would help you solve it. Be careful—there are some extras!

For #5 and #6 on the bottom, write the repeated-addition problem that could be used to solve the problem. Then solve the problem.

1. There are 7 fish in each of the 5 tanks at the pet store. How many fish are there in all?

_____

$3 + 3 + 3$

2. Tasha has 5 dolls on each of her 6 shelves. How many dolls does Tasha have?

_____

$3 + 3 + 3 + 3 + 3$

$4 + 4 + 4 + 4 + 4 + 4$

$5 + 5 + 5 + 5 + 5$

3. For the party, the 5 friends each wore 3 rings. How many rings did the friends wear altogether?

_____

$5 + 5 + 5 + 5 + 5 + 5$

$6 + 6 + 6 + 6 + 6 + 6$

4. Sam placed 4 baseball cards on 6 different pages in his album. How many cards did Sam place in his album?

_____

$6 + 6 + 6 + 6 + 6 + 6 + 6$

$7 + 7 + 7 + 7 + 7$

5. Terri placed 2 cherries on each of the 8 ice cream sundaes. How many cherries did Terri use in all? _____

6. Each of the 9 books has 3 pictures. How many pictures are there altogether? _____

Name: _____

Repeated Addition *(cont.)*

Write, Then Solve!

Directions: Write the repeated-addition problem that will help you solve the problem, and then write your answer on the line.

1. Tony has 6 quarters. How much money does Tony have?

_____

2. Amy saw 2 birds sitting on each of the 3 branches. How many birds did Amy see?

_____

3. There are 8 cookies, and each one has 4 candies on it. How many candies are there in all?

_____

4. Dad has 8 shirts for work. Each shirt has 5 buttons. How many total buttons are there?

_____

5. Janice filled 4 water balloons for each of her 6 guests. How many water balloons did Janice fill?

_____

6. If Sally reads 10 pages each night for 7 nights, how many pages will she have read?

_____

7. Jamal practiced his violin for 15 minutes 4 times this week. How many minutes did Jamal practice?

_____

8. The teacher gave each of her 23 students 3 bookmarks. How many bookmarks did the students receive?

_____

Word Problems

E
S
S
E
N
T
I
A
L

M
A
T
H
E
M
A
T
I
C
S

S
K
I
L
L
S

Skill 27: The student will solve single-step addition and subtraction word problems

Instructional Preparation

Duplicate the following (one per student, unless otherwise indicated):

- "What Should You Do?" reference sheet
- "Create the Problem" worksheet (*one per pair*)
- "Write the Sum or Difference" worksheet

Prepare an overhead transparency of the following:

- "What Should You Do?" reference sheet
- "Create the Problem" worksheet
- "Write the Sum or Difference" worksheet

Recall

Before beginning the **Review** component, facilitate a discussion based on these questions:

⁕ What is a word problem? (*a math problem that uses words to explain a situation*)

⁕ What are key words used for in solving a word problem? (*They help you decide what operation to use in solving the problem.*)

Review

1. Ask the class how many girls and boys in all are in the classroom. Ask the following question:

    ⁕ Why did you add instead of subtract? (*because the words "in all" tell you that addition is needed*)

    Explain to the students that today they will be using key words to help them solve addition and subtraction word problems.

2. Distribute the "What Should You Do?" reference sheet and display the transparency. Review the terms and definitions in the "Words to Know" section at the bottom of the page.

3. Direct attention to the top of the page. Have volunteers read the top sentence and the rest of the information in the box. Explain that key words tell how a word problem needs to be solved. Read the first problem and ask the following questions:

    ⁕ What are the key words in this problem? (*"How many more"*)

    ⁕ What operation should you use to solve this problem? (*subtraction*)

    ⁕ What is the problem that needs to be solved? (*3 − 2 = ?*)

    ⁕ What is the answer? (*1*)

    Underline the key words in the problem and write the number sentence. Continue this style of questions for problems 2 and 3. (*2. "in all" and 18 + 15 = 33; 3. "total" and 18 + 10 = 28*) Answer any questions that arise.

Word Problems *(cont.)*

Review *(cont.)*

4. Write the following sentence on the left side of the board: "There are 6 black birds and 3 brown birds on the fence." Explain that this is the beginning of a word problem. Depending on the key words used, it could be either an addition or a subtraction problem. Write this sentence underneath the first sentence: "What is the difference between the number of black birds and the number of brown birds?" Ask the following questions:

   * What key word was used? (*"difference"*)
   * What kind of word problem is this? (*subtraction*)
   * What is the problem that needs to be solved? (*6 − 3 = ?*)
   * What is the answer? (*3*)

   Rewrite the first sentence on the right side of the board: "There are 6 black birds and 3 brown birds on the fence." Write this sentence underneath it: "How many birds are on the fence in all?" Ask the following questions:

   * What key word(s) was (were) used? (*"in all"*)
   * What kind of word problem is this? (*addition*)
   * What is the problem that needs to be solved? (*6 + 3 = ?*)
   * What is the answer? (*9*)

   Divide the class into pairs. Give each pair a copy of the "Create the Problem" worksheet. Explain that on this paper are the beginnings of different story problems. Students will need to write another sentence using key words to make the problem either an addition or a subtraction problem, just like you did on the board. Tell them that they will not be solving the problems at this time, just writing the word problems. Circulate to make sure that all of the sentences written include key words for an addition or a subtraction problem. When the pairs have finished, have them exchange papers with a different pair. The pairs now need to identify the key word(s), determine whether to add or subtract, set up the number sentence, and write the answer on the appropriate lines. Circulate around the room to monitor each pair's work. When each pair has finished, have the pairs that exchanged papers sit with each other to discuss their answers. Ask for volunteers to share the sentences they wrote. Then display the "Create the Problem" transparency and have a different pair write the key word(s), operation, number sentence, and answer that belong to that problem.

5. Distribute the "Write the Sum or Difference" worksheet and display the transparency. Read the directions with the class. Have the students work on this individually. When they have finished, review the answers as a class.

Wrap-Up

To conclude this lesson, have the students write a response using complete sentences to the following prompts in their math journal or on a sheet of notebook paper. Allow adequate time for task completion and then ask various students to share their responses with the class.

   * What are some key words that tell if the problem is an addition or a subtraction problem? (*Answers may include "sum," "in all," "total," "difference," "how many more," and "left."*) Encourage the students to think of key words that were not given on the reference sheet.

   * When do you use word problems in everyday life? (*Answers will vary.*)

Word Problems *(cont.)*

What Should You Do?

Key words are words that tell how to solve a problem.

- Some key words that tell you to **add** are: *altogether, in all, total,* and *sum.*

- Some key words that tell you to **subtract** are: *left, how many more,* and *difference.*

Add or Subtract?

1. Lucy has 3 dolls with blonde hair and 2 dolls with brown hair. How many more dolls does Lucy have with blonde hair than brown hair?

_____

2. George has 18 baseball cards and 15 football cards. How many cards does George have in all?

_____

3. There are 18 white and 10 striped kittens at the pet store. How many total kittens does the pet store have?

_____

Words to Know

addition—to join together

difference—the answer to a subtraction problem

subtraction—to find the difference between two numbers

sum—the answer to an addition problem

Word Problems *(cont.)*

Create the Problem

1. Jamal has 34 racecars and 18 motorcycles.

_____

_____

What is (are) the key word(s)? _____

Should you add or subtract? _____

Write the problem. _____

What is the answer? _____

2. Tyler saw 5 dolphins and 4 sea lions at the zoo.

_____

_____

What is (are) the key word(s)? _____

Should you add or subtract? _____

Write the problem. _____

What is the answer? _____

3. There are 130 blue balloons and 100 red balloons on the stage.

_____

_____

What is (are) the key word(s)? _____

Should you add or subtract? _____

Write the problem. _____

What is the answer? _____

Word Problems *(cont.)*

Write the Sum or Difference

Directions: Underline the key word or words in each problem. Write the sum or the difference in the box.

1. Rosie took 12 pictures of her cat and 15 pictures of her dog. How many pictures altogether did Rosie take of her animals?

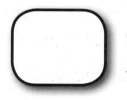

2. There were 8 monkeys in the tree and 4 monkeys on the log. How many more monkeys were in the tree than on the log?

3. Mom bought 30 large plastic cups and 15 small plastic cups for the party. How many total cups did Mom buy?

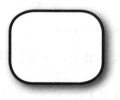

4. The library had a summer reading contest. The girls read 139 books and the boys read 128 books. What is the sum of the books the boys and girls read this summer?

5. Mrs. Simmons bought 50 pencils at the store. She gave 26 of the pencils to her students. How many pencils does Mrs. Simmons have left?

6. The gardener planted 44 flowers in the first row and 40 flowers in the second row. What is the difference between the number of flowers in the two rows?

Mathematical Terms

Skill 28: The student will use the terms *addend, sum,* and *difference.*

Instructional Preparation

Duplicate the following (one per student, unless otherwise indicated):

- "Know Your Terms!" reference sheet
- "Addition or Subtraction?" worksheet *(one per student pair)*
- "Solve It!" worksheet

Prepare an overhead transparency of the following:

- "Know Your Terms!" reference sheet
- "Addition or Subtraction?" worksheet
- "Solve It!" worksheet

Recall

Before beginning the **Review** component, facilitate a discussion based on these questions:

* Give an example of an addition problem. *(Answers will vary. Example: 4+ 2 = 6.)*

* What are some key words that are used in addition problems? *("in all," "altogether," "total," etc.)*

* Give an example of a subtraction problem. *(Answers will vary. Example: 4 − 2 = 2.)*

* What are some key words that are used in subtraction problems? *("how many more," "less than," "fewer," etc.)*

Review

1. Ask for a volunteer to count all of the boys in the class and for a different volunteer to count all of the girls in the class. Write these numbers on the board. Ask the following questions:

   * How many boys and girls are in the class altogether?

   * How many more boys than girls *(or girls than boys)* are in the class?

   Tell the class that they knew how to answer these questions because they understood the meaning of the key words and terms *altogether* and *how many more.* Explain that today they are going to use different terms that will also tell them how a problem is going to be solved.

2. Distribute the "Know Your Terms!" reference sheet and display the transparency. Direct attention to the "Words to Know" section at the bottom of the page. Review the terms and definitions with the class.

Review *(cont.)*

3. Have the class refer to the top of the page. Read the first section with the class. Ask:
   * What is the same about these three number sentences? (*They are all subtraction problems.*)
   * What is the answer to a subtraction problem called? (*the difference*)

   Explain to the class that the answer to a subtraction problem is called this because it is the difference between the two numbers.

   Direct attention to the box on the right. Ask the following questions:
   * What is the same about each of these number sentences? (*They are all addition problems.*)
   * What do you call the answer to an addition problem? (*the sum*)
   * Which numbers are addends in these problems? (*111, 34, 8, 9, 1, 4, and 3*)

   Circle the addends on the transparency as the students circle them on their papers.

   Read the first word problem with the class. Point out that the question is not asking how many bows Jenny has in all. It is asking for the difference. Ask:
   * What kind of problem is this, addition or subtraction? (*subtraction*)
   * How do you know? (*The difference is the answer to a subtraction problem.*)

   Ask for a volunteer to the read the second problem. Ask the following questions:
   * What kind of problem is this? (*addition*)
   * How do you know? (*The sum is the answer to an addition problem.*)
   * What are the 5 and the 1 in this problem called? (*addends*)

   Remind the class that when a problem tells you the kind of answer that is needed, a sum or a difference, that tells how to solve the problem.

4. Place the students in pairs. Distribute the "Addition or Subtraction?" worksheet to each pair and display the transparency. Read the directions to the first section to the students. Circulate around the room as they do this activity. When they have finished, read the directions for the second section. Monitor the pairs as they work on this section. Ask for volunteers to share their answers and mark them on the transparency. Emphasize that the terms *sum* and *difference* tell how the problems need to be solved.

5. Distribute the "Solve It!" worksheet and display the transparency. Read the directions to the students and tell them that a few of the questions have two answers. When they have completed this worksheet, discuss the answers.

Wrap-Up

To conclude this lesson, have the students write a response using complete sentences to the following prompts in their math journal or on a sheet of notebook paper. Allow adequate time for task completion and then ask various students to share their responses with the class.
   * What is an addend? (*a number that is added*)
   * What is a sum? (*the answer to an addition problem*)
   * What is a difference? (*the answer to a subtraction problem*)
   * When would you use these terms in everyday life? (*Answers will vary.*)

Mathematical Terms *(cont.)*

Know Your Terms!

Look at these number sentences. How are they alike?

4 − 3 = 1

89 − 81 = 8

300 − 14 = 286

Look at these number sentences. How are they alike?

111 + 34 = 145

8 + 9 = 17

1 + 4 + 3 = 8

1. Jenny has 4 red bows and 3 blue bows. Find the difference between the number of red bows and blue bows that Jenny has.

   What kind of problem is this? _____

   How do you know? _____

2. Peter has 5 trucks and 1 car in his backpack. Find the sum of the vehicles in Peter's backpack.

   What kind of problem is this? _____

   How do you know? _____

   What are the "5" and the "1" in this problem called? _____

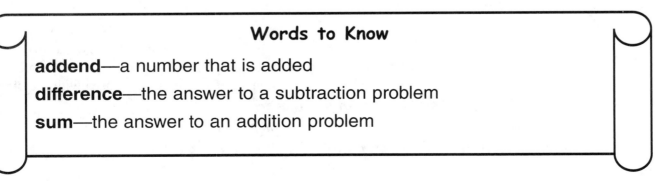

Words to Know

addend—a number that is added

difference—the answer to a subtraction problem

sum—the answer to an addition problem

Mathematical Terms *(cont.)*

Addition or Subtraction?

Directions: Draw a line from each problem to the term that describes how to solve it.

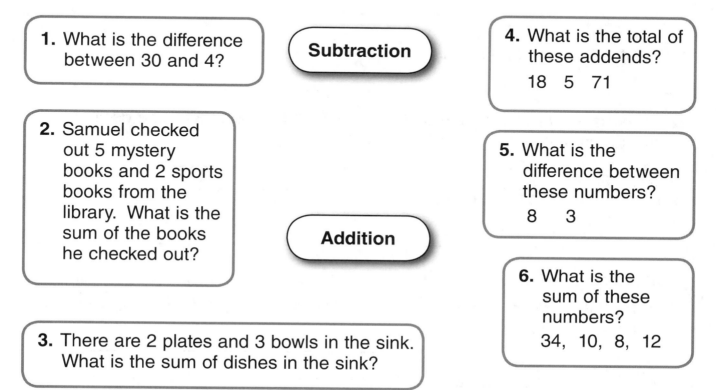

1. What is the difference between 30 and 4?

Subtraction

4. What is the total of these addends?

   18   5   71

2. Samuel checked out 5 mystery books and 2 sports books from the library. What is the sum of the books he checked out?

5. What is the difference between these numbers?

   8   3

Addition

6. What is the sum of these numbers?

   34, 10, 8, 12

3. There are 2 plates and 3 bowls in the sink. What is the sum of dishes in the sink?

Directions: Solve the problems. Write your answers on the lines.

1. What is the difference between 30 and 4? _____

2. Samuel checked out 5 mystery books and 2 sports books from the library. What is the sum of the books he checked out? _____

3. There are 2 plates and 3 bowls in the sink. What is the sum of dishes in the sink? _____

4. What is the sum of these numbers: 34, 10, 8, 12? _____

5. What is the difference between these numbers: 8 and 3? _____

6. What is the total of the addends: 18, 5, and 71? _____

Mathematical Terms *(cont.)*

Solve It!

Directions: Read each problem and write your answer on the line.

1. What is the sum of 30 and 25?

2. John just solved the problem 40 + 30 = 70. What are the addends in this problem?

3. Mandy has 12 blue balloons and 10 white balloons. What is the sum of her balloons?

4. Alex bought 25 cups for the party, and 18 of the cups were used. What is the difference between the cups that were bought and the cups that were used?

5. The pet store has 4 white and 3 brown kittens for sale. How many more white kittens than brown kittens are for sale?

   Did you find the sum or the difference?

6. The restaurant serves 14 different cold sandwiches and 7 different hot sandwiches. How many sandwiches do they serve in all?

   Did you find the sum or the difference?

7. Mom bought 10 rose bushes and 5 vines at the nursery. How many total plants did Mom buy?

   Did you find the sum or the difference?

PAL Packets

Introduction

PAL Packets are an important component of the *Essential Skills* series. PAL stands for "Parent Assisted Learning," and each PAL Packet lesson is meant to supplement student learning with a short activity that gives parents and guardians the tools to help their children practice important skills.

The following lessons can be found in both English and Spanish on the CDs that accompany this book. A sample PAL lesson has been provided in both English and Spanish in the pages that follow.

Approximate Size of Units of Length, Capacity, and Weight ✳ *Learn how to select the appropriate unit of measurement for lengths, capacities, and weights.*

Congruence ✳ *Learn how to recognize congruent forms.*

Extraneous Information ✳ *Learn to determine the information needed to solve word problems that contain extra information.*

Find a Missing Number in a Pattern ✳ *Learn to find missing numbers in a pattern.*

Fractions ✳ *Learn how to relate common fractions to pictures.*

Locate and Name Points on a Line ✳ *Learn how to locate and name points oon a number line.*

Make or Use a Table or Graph to Represent and Analyze Data ✳ *Learn how to use graph to make comparisons, indentifications, and predictions.*

Measure to Solve Problems ✳ *Learn to choose the correct units to measure length and distance.*

Order Numbers ✳ *Learn to put numbers in order.*

Represent Problems with Number Sentences ✳ *Learn to read word problems and select the number sentence that represents the math problem in them.*

Symmetry and Congruency ✳ *Learn about figures that have the same size and shape or that can be divided into identical halves.*

Translate Between Words and Symbols in Naming Whole Numbers ✳ *Learn to read and write number values as words and symbols.*

Use a Thermometer ✳ *Learn to use a thermometer to measure temperature.*

P
A
L

P
A
C
K
E
T

Parent Assisted Learning (PAL)

Mathematics
Grade 3
Extraneous Information

P A L   P A C K E T

Dear Parent or Guardian:

Your child is currently learning to solve word problems that include extra information. Here is your chance to help your child practice this important skill.

In this PAL Packet you will find a short activity for you and your child to do. Please do the activity and "The Back Page." Then sign your name on "The Back Page" and have your child return it by _____.

Thanks for your help.

Sincerely,

_____

Needed Information

Parent Pointer

How often have you said, "I don't need to know all that information"? If you want to send a card, all you need is the address. You do not need to know on which side of the street the house is located, the house's size and color, or if the yard is fenced. Learning how to determine the information needed to solve a problem that contains extra information is important for your child in developing problem-solving and reasoning skills.

Student Directions

Ask your parent or guardian to read and talk about the information in the "Parent Pointer" with you. Then, follow the directions and complete the activity in finding the information needed to solve the word problems on the "Mystery Message" pages with your parent or guardian.

Talk About It

After you have finished the activity, go to "The Back Page" to show what you know.

Now go have some fun with the activity!

Mystery Message

P A L   P A C K E T

Directions:

- Read the word problem.

- Read the first sentence under the word problem. Is this information needed to solve the problem? Yes. So a ✔ was made in the box next to the O in the "Needed" column.

Now it's your turn!

With your parent or partner:

- Read the next sentence.

- Make a ✔ next to the letter in the "Needed" column if you need to know that information to solve the problem.

- Solve the problem and write the answer on the line

- Follow these directions to complete problems A and B.

A. You ride your blue bike a mile to the store to buy an energy bar for 50¢ and a fruit drink for 75¢. You have $1.50. Do you have enough money to buy an energy bar and a fruit drink?

		Needed
Your energy bar costs 50¢.	O	✔
You ride a mile to the store.	A	☐
The fruit drink costs 75¢.	Y	✔
You have $1.50.	U	✔
Your bike is blue.	L	☐

Do you have enough money? _____**Yes**_____

Mystery Message (cont.)

B. On the way to the store, you stop and talk to 5 friends. At the store you see 3 friends. On the way home from the store, you eat your energy bar, drink your fruit juice, adjust the chain on your bike, and wave to 6 more friends. How many friends did you see altogether?

		Needed
You talked to 5 friends.	I	☐
You see 3 friends at the store.	N	☐
You ate your energy bar.	P	☐
You adjusted the chain on your bike.	R	☐
You waved to 6 more friends.	W	☐

How many friends did you see? _____

In the mystery message box below, write the letter from each box that has a checkmark in it from problems A and B.

Letter Box [   ]

Now, *unscramble* the letters and write them on the lines below to find out the mystery message!

MYSTERY MESSAGE: ____ ____ ____   ____ ____ ____ !

Way to go! You have great problem-solving skills!

The Back Page

Talk About It

Parent ➤ Ask your son or daughter the following question:

- How would you explain needed and extra information in a word problem to a friend?

Student ➤ Answer the above question in complete sentences.

_____

_____

_____

_____

_____

➤ **Do one of the following activities on a separate piece of paper:**

- Write a short word problem with at least two pieces of needed and two pieces of extra information for your parent or guardian to solve.

- Write a short word problem with needed and extra information and draw a picture of what is happening in the problem. Circle the part of the drawing that shows the needed information. Solve the problem.

_____   _____
Student's Name   *Parent or Guardian's Signature*

Parent Assisted Learning (PAL)

Mathematics
Grade 3
Extraneous Information

PAL PACKET

Estimado padre/madre o tutor legal:

Actualmente su hijo/a está aprendiendo a resolver problemas que incluyen información extra. Esta es su oportunidad para ayudarle a practicar esta importante habilidad.

En este paquete PAL encontrará una actividad corta para hacer junto con su hijo/a. Favor de hacer la actividad y "La última página." Después firme "La última página" y mándela con su hijo/a el día _____.

Gracias por su ayuda.

Atentamente,

_____

P
A
L

P
A
C
K
E
T

Información necesaria

Consejo para los padres

¿Cuántas veces ha dicho: «No necesito saber tanta información»? Si quiere mandar una carta, la única cosa que necesita es la dirección. No necesita saber en qué lado de la calle está la casa, el tamaño de la casa ni color o si el jardín tiene una cerca. Aprender a determinar la información necesaria para resolver un problema que contiene información extra es importante para desarrollar las habilidades de resolver problemas y razonar.

Instrucciones para el estudiante

Pídale a su padre/madre o tutor legal que lea y hable con usted sobre la información en "Consejo para los padres". Entonces, siga las instrucciones con su padre/madre o tutor legal para terminar la actividad de encontrar la información que se necesita para resolver los problemas en las páginas "Mensaje misterioso."

Hablen sobre la actividad

Después de terminar la actividad, pasen a "La última página" para mostrar lo que sabe.

¡Ahora diviértanse con la actividad!

Mensaje misterioso

Instrucciones:

- Lea el problema de palabras.

- Lea la primera oración debajo del problema de palabras. ¿Es necesaria esta información para resolver el problema? Sí. Por eso, un ✔ está en la caja al lado de la columna "Necesario".

¡Ahora le toca a Usted!

Con su padre/madre o tutor legal:

- Lea la siguiente oración.

- Ponga ✔ al lado de la letra en la columna "Necesario" si necesita saber esa información para resolver el problema.

- Resuelva el problema y escriba la respuesta en la línea.

- Siga estas instrucciones para completar los problemas A y B.

A. En su bicicleta azul, usted va a la tienda para comprar una barra de energía por 50¢ y un jugo de fruta por 75¢. Usted tiene $1.50. ¿Tiene suficiente dinero para una barra de energía y un jugo de fruta?

                                                  Necesario

Su barra de energía cuesta 50¢.	O	☐
Monta en bicicleta una milla a la tienda.	A	☐
El jugo cuesta 75¢.	Y	☐
Usted tiene $1.50.	U	☐
Su bicicleta es azul.	L	☐

- ¿Tiene suficiente dinero? _____

P A L P A C K E T

Información extra

Mensaje misterioso (continuación)

B. En ruta a la tienda, se para y habla con 5 amigos. En la tienda ve a 3 amigos. Regresando a casa, se come su barra de energía, se toma el jugo de fruta, ajusta la cadena de la bicicleta y saluda a 6 amigos más. ¿Cuántos amigos vio en total?

	¿Necesario?
Habla con 5 amigos.	I ☐
Ve a 3 amigos en la tienda.	N ☐
Se come la barra de energía.	P ☐
Ajusta la cadena de la bicicleta.	R ☐
Saluda a 6 amigos.	W ☐

¿Cuántos amigos vio en total? _____

En la caja con el mensaje misterioso abajo, escriba la letra de cada caja que tenga un en los problemas A y B.

Caja de letras [_____]

¡Ahora, *descifre* las letras y escríbalas en las líneas a continuación para encontrar el mensaje (en Inglés)!

MENSAJE MISTERIOSO: ___ ___ ___ ___ ___ ___ !

¡Bien! ¡Tiene muy buena habilidad para resolver problemas!

#6213 ES: Math

172

©Teacher Created Resources, Inc.

La última página

Hablen sobre la actividad

Padre/madre ➤ Haga a su hijo/a la siguiente pregunta:

- ¿Cómo explicaría información necesaria y información extra en un problema a un amigo?

Estudiante ➤ Conteste la pregunta anterior con oraciones completas en el espacio que sigue.

_____

_____

_____

_____

_____

_____

➤ **Haga una de las siguientes actividades en una hoja de papel:**

- Escriba un problema de palabras corto con por lo menos dos ejemplos de información necesaria y dos ejemplos de información extra para que lo resuelva su padre/madre o tutor legal.

- Escriba un problema de palabras corto de información necesaria e información extra y haga un dibujo de lo que está pasando en el problema. Encierre en un círculo la parte del dibujo que demuestra la información necesaria. Resuelva el problema.

_____ _____
Nombre del estudiante   *Firma del padre/madre o tutor legal*

Answer Key

Rules, page 10

1. Add 20   2. Add 10   3. Subtract 5

4.

Rule: Add 25	
200	225
250	275
300	325
350	375
400	425

5.

Rule: Subtract 4					
19	18	17	16	15	14
15	14	13	12	11	10

6.

Rule: Double, Subtract 2	
9	16
20	38
21	40
25	48
33	64
40	78
41	80

Patterns in Tables, page 11

1.

112	127
122	137
132	147
142	157
152	167

Add 15

2.

51	56
53	58
67	72
69	74
74	79
77	82

Add 5

3.

30	33	36	39	42
34	37	40	43	46

Add 4

4.

417	397	377	357	337
406	386	366	346	326

Subtract 11

5.

93	92	91	90	89	88
86	85	84	83	82	337

Subtract 7

6.

15	27
17	29
19	31
21	33
23	35

Add 12

I Understand Number Patterns!, page 18

1. add 4, subtract 2
2. 110, 90, 70
3. 94
4. subtract 6
5. Answers will vary. Example: 3, 18, 33, 48, 63, 78.
6. Answers will vary. Example: 100, 96, 92, 88, 84, 80.

What Does It Show?, pages 27–28

1. Ice Pops Sold
3. 46
3. cherry, grape, and orange
4. 52 minutes
5. the different subjects
6. 8 minutes
7. 3 animals
8. 9
9. jackets
10. T-shirts
11. 12
12. 3

Circle It, Draw It, Write It, page 33

1. shapes 1, 5, 8
2.

3. figures having the same shape and size
4. one that has two matching halves

I Know My Figures!, page 39

1.

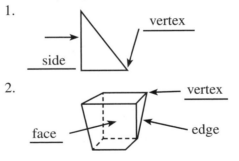

2.

3. 3-D; 8 vertices, 6 faces, 12 edges

Answer Key *(cont.)*

4. 3-D; 5 vertices, 5 faces, 8 edges
5. 2-D; 5 vertices, 5 sides
6. 3-D; 8 vertices, 6 faces, 12 edges

Which Unit Is It?, pages 44–45
1. 20 gallons
2. 15 miles
3. 15 pounds
4. 3 milliliters
5. 5 liters
6. 3 kilometers
7. 3 kilograms
8. 50 pounds

Number of units will vary; accept all reasonable answers.

9. 6 centimeters
10. 6 inches
11. 1 cup
12. 2 grams
13. 10 feet

Choose the Unit, page 46
1. 8 inches
2. 12 pounds
3. 1 ounce
4. 2 cups
5. 40 meters
6. 2 grams
7. 4 milliliters
8. 2 feet

Choose the Measurement Tool, page 51
1. tape measure
2. clock
3. thermometer
4. gallon container
5. scale
6. calendar
7. measuring cup
8. clock

How Much?, page 59
1. Sandra has $6.42.
2. Zack has 42¢, and Terri has 38¢. Terri has less money.
3. Jerry found $1.12.
4. Tony has 51¢, and Jan has 46¢. Tony received more change.
5. $2.81
6. Betty earned $22.95, Kyle earned $20.90, and Juan earned $22.90. Betty earned the most money.

Find the Time, page 64
1. 13 hours
2. 1:00
3. 10:00
4. 11 hours
5. 6 hours
6. 2:00

The Time Is . . ., page 65
1. 10:00
2. 4 hours
3. 6:00
4. 1 hour
5. 2:00
6. 3 hours
7. 11:00
8. 12:00

What's Missing?, page 70
1. Saturday
2. January
3. June, August
4. Monday, Thursday
5. April
6. July, August
7. Monday, Thursday
8. Thursday, Friday, Sunday

Situations, page 75
1. a.m.
2. p.m.
3. a.m.
4. p.m.
5. p.m.
6. p.m.
7. p.m.
8. p.m.
9. a.m.
10. a.m.

A.M. or P.M.?, page 76
1. 5:30 p.m.
2. 10:30 a.m.
3. 11:45 p.m.
6. 9:10 p.m.
7. p.m. Times will vary.
8. Times will vary.

4. 8:30 p.m.
5. 5:25 a.m.
9. 12:10 p.m.
10. 1:05 a.m.

Money—It's All $ and ¢, page 82
1. $8.42
2. $0.91, 91¢
3. $1.01
4. $3.23
5. 4¢, $0.04
6. $18.00
7. $0.17, 17¢
8. $3.04
9. $10.80
10. $0.24, 24¢
11. $6.16

Heads or Tails, page 87
addition answer; subtraction answer
1. 912; 648
2. 602; 508
3. 2,901; 2,707
4. 787; 199
5. 54; 24
6. 400; 224
7. 136; 38
8. 8,505; 8,143
9. 1,339; 525
10. 120; 26
11. 1,197; 89
12. 318; 144

Watch the Signs!, page 88
1. 530
2. 112
3. 4,299
4. 706
5. 270
6. 7,131
7. 8,665
8. 39
9. 189
10. 14
11. 289
12. 47

A Family of Facts, page 92
1. 114 − 21 = 93
2. 221 − 116 = 105
3. 60 − 15 = 45
4. 19 + 10 = 29; 10 + 19 = 29; 29 − 10 = 19; 29 − 19 = 10
5. 3 + 7 = 10; 10 − 7 = 3; 7 + 3 = 10; 10 − 3 = 7
6. 959 − 831 = 128
7. 49 + 37 = 86; 86 − 49 = 37
8. 90 − 59 = 31; 31 + 59 = 90; 59 + 31 = 90

Fact Families and Inverses, page 93
1. 83 − 68 = 15 or 83 − 15 = 68
2. 44 − 31 = 13, 13 + 31 = 44, 31 + 13 = 44
3. 1,100 + 3,756 = 4,856
4. 500 + 5 = 505 or 5 + 500 = 505
5. No, Sam is not correct. A fact family always uses the same three numbers.
6. Answers will vary.

Add 10, Subtract 10, page 97
1. 67, 77, 87
2. 350, 360, 370
3. 191, 201, 211
4. 27, 37, 47
5. 519, 529, 539
6. 33, 23, 13
7. 682, 672, 662
8. 278, 268, 258
9. 400, 390, 380

10 Is the Number, page 98
1. 71
2. 97
3. 155
4. 121
5. 408
6. 82
7. 2
8. 796
9. 459
10. 35

What Fraction Is Shaded?, page 102
1. ¼
2. 2/3
3. 4/8
4. 3/4

Answer Key *(cont.)*

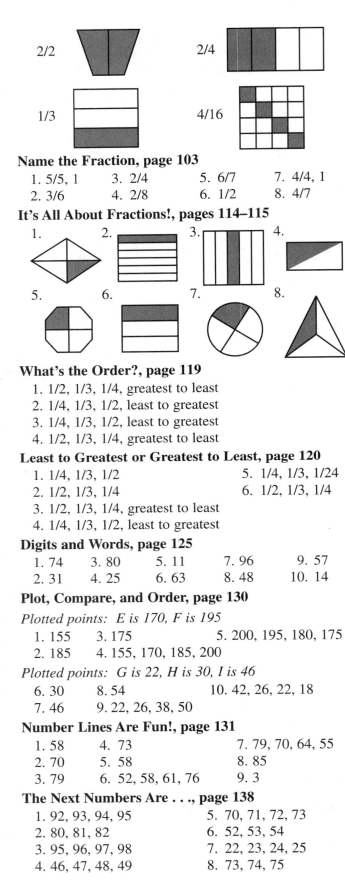

2/2   2/4

1/3   4/16

Name the Fraction, page 103

1. 5/5, 1   3. 2/4   5. 6/7   7. 4/4, 1
2. 3/6   4. 2/8   6. 1/2   8. 4/7

It's All About Fractions!, pages 114–115

1.   2.   3.   4.

5.   6.   7.   8.

What's the Order?, page 119

1. 1/2, 1/3, 1/4, greatest to least
2. 1/4, 1/3, 1/2, least to greatest
3. 1/4, 1/3, 1/2, least to greatest
4. 1/2, 1/3, 1/4, greatest to least

Least to Greatest or Greatest to Least, page 120

1. 1/4, 1/3, 1/2   5. 1/4, 1/3, 1/24
2. 1/2, 1/3, 1/4   6. 1/2, 1/3, 1/4
3. 1/2, 1/3, 1/4, greatest to least
4. 1/4, 1/3, 1/2, least to greatest

Digits and Words, page 125

1. 74   3. 80   5. 11   7. 96   9. 57
2. 31   4. 25   6. 63   8. 48   10. 14

Plot, Compare, and Order, page 130

Plotted points: E is 170, F is 195

1. 155   3. 175   5. 200, 195, 180, 175
2. 185   4. 155, 170, 185, 200

Plotted points: G is 22, H is 30, I is 46

6. 30   8. 54   10. 42, 26, 22, 18
7. 46   9. 22, 26, 38, 50

Number Lines Are Fun!, page 131

1. 58   4. 73   7. 79, 70, 64, 55
2. 70   5. 58   8. 85
3. 79   6. 52, 58, 61, 76   9. 3

The Next Numbers Are . . ., page 138

1. 92, 93, 94, 95   5. 70, 71, 72, 73
2. 80, 81, 82   6. 52, 53, 54
3. 95, 96, 97, 98   7. 22, 23, 24, 25
4. 46, 47, 48, 49   8. 73, 74, 75

Write It Differently!, page 142

13 + 4; 18 − 1   18 − 12; 6
7; 3 + 1 + 3   19; 10 + 4 + 5
20 − 5; 16 − 1   2 + 4 + 6 + 4; 10 + 6
4 + 8 + 1; 15 − 2

For the bottom section, answers will vary. The following are examples:

1. 3 + 4   3. 9 + 9   5. 5 + 1
2. 2 + 3   4. 7 + 7   6. 20 − 4

Match It, Write It, Solve It!, page 149

1. 7 + 7 + 7 + 7 + 7
2. 5 + 5 + 5 + 5 + 5 + 5
3. 3 + 3 + 3 + 3 + 3
4. 4 + 4 + 4 + 4 + 4 + 4
5. 2 + 2 + 2 + 2 + 2 + 2 + 2 + 2 = 16 or 8 + 8 = 16
6. 3 + 3 + 3 + 3 + 3 + 3 + 3 + 3 + 3 = 27 or
   9 + 9 + 9 = 27

Write, Then Solve!, page 150

1. $0.25 + $0.25 + $0.25 + $0.25 + $0.25 + $0.25 or
   6 + 6 + 6 + 6 + 6 + 6 + 6 + 6 + 6 + 6 + 6 + 6 + 6
   + 6 + 6 + 6 + 6 + 6 + 6 + 6 + 6 + 6 + 6 + 6 + 6.
   Tony has $1.50.
2. 2 + 2 + 2 or 3 + 3. Amy saw 6 birds.
3. 4 + 4 + 4 + 4 + 4 + 4 + 4 + 4 or 8 + 8 + 8 + 8.
   There are 32 candies.
4. 5 + 5 + 5 + 5 + 5 + 5 + 5 + 5 or 8 + 8 + 8 + 8 + 8.
   Dad has 40 buttons on his shirts.
5. 4 + 4 + 4 + 4 + 4 + 4 or 6 + 6 + 6 + 6. Janice
   filled 24 balloons.
6. 10 + 10 + 10 + 10 + 10 + 10 + 10 or 7 + 7 + 7 + 7
   + 7 + 7 + 7 + 7 + 7 + 7. Sally will read 70 pages.
7. 15 + 15 + 15 + 15 or 4 + 4 + 4 + 4 + 4 + 4 + 4 +
   4 + 4 + 4 + 4 + 4 + 4 + 4 + 4. Jamal practiced 60
   minutes, or 1 hour.
8. 3 + 3 + 3 + 3 + 3 + 3 + 3 + 3 + 3 + 3 + 3 + 3 + 3
   + 3 + 3 + 3 + 3 + 3 + 3 + 3 + 3 + 3 + 3 or 23 + 23
   + 23. The students received 69 bookmarks.

Write the Sum or Difference, page 155

1. "altogether"; 27   4. "sum"; 267
2. "how many more"; 4   5. "have left"; 24
3. "total"; 45   6. "difference"; 4

Addition or Subtraction?, page 159

Subtraction: 1, 5

Addition: 2, 3, 4, 6

1. 26   2. 7   3. 5   4. 64   5. 5   6. 94

Solve It!, page 160

1. 55   4. 7   6. 21; sum
2. 40 and 30   5. 1; difference   7. 15; sum
3. 22